THE COMPLETE IRONMAN®

THIS IS A CARLTON BOOK

Published by Carlton Books Ltd
20 Mortimer Street
London W1T 3JW

For more brand information, please visit www.IRONMAN.com
IRONMAN® and the "M-DOT" logo are registered trademarks of World Triathlon Corporation. Official Product of the IRONMAN® TRIATHLON. Used here by permission.

ISBN 978-1-78097-988-5

Editorial Manager: Chris Mitchell
Design Manager: Andri Johannsson
Design: www.fogdog.co.uk
Production: Ena Matagic
Picture Research: Paul Langan

A CIP catalogue for this book is available from the British Library

Printed in Italy

10 9 8 7 6 5 4 3 2 1

THE COMPLETE

IRONMAN®

THE OFFICIAL ILLUSTRATED GUIDE TO THE ULTIMATE ENDURANCE RACE

C

CARLTON
BOOKS

◄ Patrick Lange celebrates
becoming the 2017
IRONMAN World Champion,
breaking the course record
in the process.

CONTENTS

FOREWORD BY ANDREW MESSICK

This is a very exciting year for us here at IRONMAN. Through celebrating our 40th anniversary – a milestone we've named "40 Years of Dreams" – we've had the opportunity to express gratitude, to reminisce, and to dream. Many athletes, communities, partners, staff, and volunteers have shaped our history and helped pave the way for others to fulfill their potential by crossing one of our life-changing finish lines.

From the very first race on the shores of O'ahu, Hawai`i in 1978, IRONMAN has carved out a unique legacy in sports history. This is largely due to our extraordinary athletes and the hundreds of thousands of unforgettable journeys they have shared with us. This year, we are proud to mark four decades of IRONMAN athletes proving that "Anything is Possible".

This book tells the story not only of our races, but of our community. You will learn about the history of this unique sport, and you will be introduced to a cast of characters who helped bring us to where we are today. We trust that you will find something encouraging and inspiring in these pages.

As we continue to grow around the world, we hold tightly to the ideals that launched that very first challenge in 1978.

On behalf of all of us at IRONMAN, thank you for being part of our family.

Andrew Messick
President and Chief Executive Officer, IRONMAN

▶ Gordon Ramsay before his first IRONMAN World Championship race in October 2013.

FOREWORD BY GORDON RAMSAY

The race of a lifetime... I finished the IRONMAN® World Championship in Kailua-Kona, Hawai`i, in 2013.

I spent months training: I would leap up at 4am to dive into the pool three days a week, followed by two-hour sessions on the bike; in between, I took on 6–12 mile runs on Tuesdays and Thursdays, and then a long-distance run on Saturdays... Sundays were a much-appreciated rest day.

I'll never forget stepping off that plane in Hawai`i. So many emotions. Up until that point I had completed 15 marathons, three ultra-marathons, and three IRONMAN 70.3® races. But now I was getting ready to do the world's toughest IRONMAN competition!

There's nothing else quite like it. When race day comes, you're up at 3am, and if you're like me then you couldn't fall asleep until after 11pm the night before. I was just too damn excited for what was to come. The swim at the start of the race is an extraordinary moment, it is just so surprisingly quiet. The starting cannon for the pros goes off, and you can hear every age-grouper's footsteps in the sand, pounding away as they move towards the water. You're thinking, "This is insane," but then before you know it hours have gone by as you chip away at a 2.4-mile swim, 112-mile bike ride and 26.2-mile run.

As I looked around, taking in the scenery, surrounded by amazing athletes, I was inspired to keep going and finish what I had come to accomplish. And whether it is your first, your second, or even your fifth race, there's an unspeakable bond between all of the finishers. We support one another, before, during and after.

When you cross that finish line, soaking wet, out of breath, thirsty, hungry, in pain and utterly exhausted, you are suddenly empowered. There's nothing quite as gratifying. And already, I'm thinking about my next race.

Gordon x

▶ The spectacular swim start at Kona during the 2016 IRONMAN World Championship.

INTRODUCTION BY BOB BABBITT

Back in 1977, US Naval Commander John Collins and his wife Judy had already participated in some of the early triathlons run in San Diego, California, at the start of the decade. Having moved to O'ahu, Hawai`i, they put out a challenge to a group of friends that eventually led to the creation of the IRONMAN® triathlon.

▲ Bob Babbitt at the third IRONMAN race in 1980. The event had grown from 15 starters to 108 by this point.

An article had been published in *Sports Illustrated* insisting that cyclist Eddy Merckx, the five-time winner of the Tour de France, was the world's best endurance athlete. At the awards dinner for the Perimeter Relay, an open-water swim race in O'ahu, people started discussing who was actually the world's fittest. Some felt a hypothetical swimmer or runner would be the best endurance athlete over a cyclist. Commander Collins and his wife, who had both participated in shorter swim, bike and run events in San Diego in the mid-1970s, decided to go to the stage and take the microphone.

"We'll start with the 2.4-mile Waikiki Rough Water Swim," they said, "and follow that up with the Around O'ahu Bike Ride, which is 112 miles, and then finish up with the 26.2-mile Honolulu Marathon. We'll call the winner the IRONMAN."

At that first IRONMAN race on February 18, 1978, there were only 15 brave souls, including John Collins, standing in the sand of Sans Souci Beach to see if it was actually possible to swim, bike and run 140.6 miles all in one day. The first-ever IRONMAN champion was taxi driver Gordon Haller, who finished in 11:46:40.

In the 40 years since John and Judy announced their new event – combining three of the toughest existing endurance races on the island of O'ahu – the IRONMAN® World Championship has become the most important one-day endurance event on the planet. Thousands of people dedicate their lives to trying to earn a qualifying spot in the championship, which is now held in Kailua-Kona, Hawai`i each October.

The IRONMAN brand has grown to include more than 150 IRONMAN and IRONMAN 70.3® events over 55 countries around the world. From 15 starters to hundreds of thousands, the desire for people from all walks of life to become an IRONMAN is stronger now than it has ever been. This book will take you on a journey through time and share the history, the training and the classic moments of what has become an international phenomenon.

If you are actually lucky enough to reach that iconic IRONMAN finish line on Ali'i Drive, one thing is guaranteed: your life will be changed forever.

Bob Babbitt
IRONMAN Hall of Fame Inductee

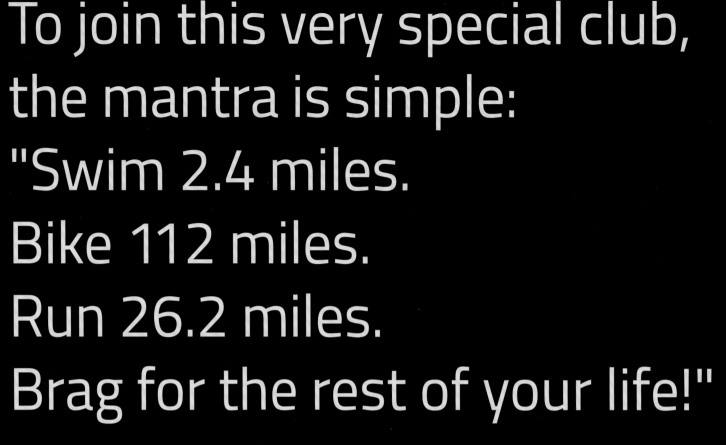

To join this very special club, the mantra is simple:
"Swim 2.4 miles.
Bike 112 miles.
Run 26.2 miles.
Brag for the rest of your life!"
– John Collins, IRONMAN founder

▶ The start of a life-changing day for the athletes at IRONMAN South Africa in Port Elizabeth.

THE HISTORY OF
IRONMAN

A 2.4-mile swim, 112-mile bike, and 26.2-mile run are feats unto themselves; to complete all three in less than 17 hours? That takes something special. The first IRONMAN race took place in 1978 and even then it was possible to see what IRONMAN would become: the most challenging single-day sporting event in the world, and the proof of the belief that "Anything is Possible".

◀ IRONMAN athletes charge towards the water at the start of the IRONMAN 70.3 Mallorca.

Around the world, there are a variety of triathlons that take place over many different distances. The 140.6 miles of an IRONMAN race, however, is regarded as the pinnacle of the sport. Since its inception in 1978, IRONMAN has developed beyond the full distance and launched, or embraced, a number of other race distances such as the half distance, or IRONMAN 70.3®. There is no doubt, though, that for the hundreds of thousands of athletes who take part in IRONMAN events every year, the magical number of 140.6 miles is the ultimate goal.

Short course triathlon was recognized on the world stage when the Olympics adopted the event at the Sydney Games in a shortened format: a 0.93 mile swim, 24.8 mile bike, and 6.2 mile run. Long course triathlon was born in Hawai`i as the result of a light-hearted debate in 1977 between a number of fitness fanatics – including husband and wife John and Judy Collins.

This might at first appear to be an unlikely venue. The fiftieth and most recent state in America, the home of the colorful *lei* garland and the graceful *hula* dance is more usually known for embodying tranquility, beauty and relaxation among its awe-inspiring geography and restful blue seas. This is not a place that is normally associated with having to find every last iota of strength just to take the next step. But this is where elite athletes and determined amateurs alike can be found – men and women, able-bodied and physically challenged – straining each muscle and battling heat and trade winds to complete the world's toughest test.

So Hawai`i is where it all began. John Collins, then a U.S. Navy Commander, and his wife Judy, had the idea for what would become IRONMAN at the award ceremony for a relay race in O`ahu, the most populous of the eight islands that make up Hawai`i. It was 1977, and the couple was sitting with their swimming friends arguing over who were the better athletes – swimmers or runners. John suggested that bicyclists also ought to be considered, as he had just read "that Eddy Merckx had the highest O_2 uptake" (now called VO_2 max). There were already Hawaiian events in all three disciplines and John thought that they could be combined into one mega-race. It was, at the very least, one way of resolving the argument.

Just south of Honolulu lies Waikiki Bay, the site of the Waikiki Roughwater Swim, which covered 2.4 miles. This, Collins thought, could be used to lead into the course of the existing Round the Island Bike Race – a 115-mile event that was previously staged over two days. Collins would take off three miles from that second event to include it in the one-day spectacular. Participants would next end up at the start of the Honolulu Marathon, which had first been run in 1973 and, like the Waikiki competition, is still going today. John took to the stage that night and made his suggestion.

"I said the gun would go off and the clock would keep running and whoever finished first, well, we'd call him the IRONMAN," he later explained. "It got a really good laugh at the time." There would, no doubt have been a bigger laugh had anyone thought to claim that the IRONMAN would go on to be a global phenomenon run by hundreds of thousands each year. Over the next 40 years, it would grow to be supported by an increasing number of corporate sponsors, with televised coverage of events reaching across the globe. Impossible to imagine as it was at the time, all of this would

▼ John and Judy Collins on a training run. John is wearing his original 1978 IRONMAN finisher t-shirt.

▲ Waikiki Bay, the site of the Waikiki Roughwater Swim and the starting point for the very first IRONMAN triathlon in 1978.

happen, and more. Over the years, the challenge would transform countless lives and change the reputation of endurance sports.

If anyone was qualified to bring such an unlikely event to life, it was the Collins family. The whole family already had triathlon experience; they were involved from the very early days of the modern incarnation of the event. Triathlon had originated in the early 1970s as a way of breaking up the monotony of run training. At the time, the Collinses lived in Coronado, just over the bay from downtown San Diego, California. Some of the first triathlons were held nearby in Mission Bay and in 1974, John and Judy, both then in their thirties, participated in the events. Their children –

Kristin and Michael, then aged 13 and 12, respectively – also took part. The following year, the couple and their friends organized their own triathlon in Coronado, before the Navy relocated the Collins family to Hawai`i. Across the Pacific from that southwestern U.S. home of triathlon, their passion for sport remained undimmed. Enthusiastic about the latest idea to stage this gigantic triathlon, local friends joined the Collinses in O'ahu.

The first IRONMAN triathlon was a family affair. The Collinses designed and assembled the trophies and created the logo, which was printed on t-shirts the 15 participants provided themselves. John's briefing included a handwritten note: "Swim 2.4 miles. Bike 112

(*From left to right*) John, Michael, Judy and Kristin Collins on the beach after the Waikiki Roughwater Swim in 1976.

▲▲ The athletes gather to hear last-minute instructions before the first IRONMAN triathlon.

▲ The article written about Gordon Haller's victory by Dick Fishback in the *Honolulu Advertiser* on February 10, 1978.

place at that point was John Dunbar, who went on to transition from the cycling portion with a 13-minute lead over Gordon Haller, a taxi driver by trade. But Haller eventually took the overall lead late in the marathon thanks to his time of 3:30 – including stops to combat cramps. Haller went on to be the very first IRONMAN winner, with an overall time of 11:46:40. Both of the Collins' had originally planned to take part; although Judy had to drop out just days before, John came in at just over 17 hours. Writing in the *Honolulu Advertiser* on the day after the race, Dick Fishback – who was still recovering from his original assumption that the events would be held separately over three days – commented, "If there was ever a case of mind over matter, it was tried yesterday." Over the years, the IRONMAN World Championship has seen many incredible feats from the athletes. These are fully detailed in The 40 Greatest IRONMAN World Championship Moments chapter.

miles. Run 26 miles. Brag for the rest of your life!" Local gym Nautilus Fitness Center gave competitor Gordon Haller free membership and training in return for the publicity. That IRONMAN race took place in Waikiki Bay on February 18, 1978, and concluded with just 12 finishers.

Archie Hapai was the early leader as the competitors finished their swim. In second

IRONMAN IN PRINT

IRONMAN was an immediate success, in that it generated word-of-mouth interest. Yet, as it moved towards its second edition, there was still nothing to indicate it would one day become such a global phenomenon. There was no prize money awarded, and John Collins took a slight loss on staging the inaugural competition. Only down $25, he decided to keep going. The second outing of the event promised to boost the field by more than double; and Nautilus Fitness, run by husband-and-wife team Hank Grundman and Valerie Silk, provided funding and volunteers to help the race. After bad weather delayed the start by a day, by the time it finally began there were just 15 competitors there to take on the challenge again. They included Lyn Lemaire, a cyclist from Boston, Massachusetts, and the first female IRONMAN finisher, and San Diego resident, Tom Warren, who took overall first place with a time of 11:15:56. John Collins was keen to encourage more people to take part and considered changing the race to a relay as one way of attracting more competitors. But then Warren's win was written up in a major magazine, *Sports Illustrated*.

Writer Barry McDermott had stumbled across IRONMAN while on assignment in Hawai`i for the publication to cover a golf tournament. He put together a vivid ten-page account of the key characters, their larger-than-life routines and the challenges they faced, which was published in May 1979. The resulting publicity created a buzz about this extraordinary new competition that straightforward advertising could never have matched. Warren became a minor celebrity as a result, while Collins was inundated with hundreds of letters from people all over the world who wanted to know how they could sign up. It was clear that the stories of the IRONMAN pioneers resonated with ordinary people.

The attraction was not hard to fathom; these early IRONMAN competitors were a new breed. They weren't like the more conventional athletes who dominated just one particular discipline. These were heroes that anyone could aspire to be. When Warren had first toured the marathon course as part of his preparation, he came across a restaurant with a wooden carved lion outside for sale. It stood over three feet tall and would be expensive to ship home, but he promised himself the brave creature if he won. When he was awarded his trophy, the organizers asked if he needed anything else. He asked them to take him back to the restaurant,

◄ Lyn Lemaire – an American champion cyclist and the first female IRONMAN finisher – shortly before starting the 1979 IRONMAN triathlon.

where he bought what turned out to be the start of a collection of hundreds of carvings. This was exactly the sort of personality it took to triumph over the tests of an IRONMAN race.

"I guess I have an obsessive-compulsive nature," Warren later admitted, although his training just weeks before the race only encompassed a mile in a pool, a 40-mile ride, and a 6-mile run. But this was the same person who had traveled from San Diego to Las Vegas for vacation – by bike. He cycled 360 miles over desert territory in baking heat, while his girlfriend and friends traveled separately by car.

IRONMAN, it was clear, wasn't so much about admiring athletic perfection from afar as it was taking part with a toughness and dogged determination to make it to the finish line. The original story of the IRONMAN competitor was one of eccentricity, individualism and a fierce drive. McDermott's piece captured a drama that any reader could identify with.

In addition to the letters that followed the *Sports Illustrated* piece came a request from ABC Sports, a national TV network, to film the following year's event. Collins agreed, telling ABC that they had to bring their own crew and cover any expenses themselves. For once,

◀ Valerie Silk, under whose stewardship the IRONMAN World Championship grew from a 326-person race in 1981 to a triathlon involving thousands of athletes from all around the world.

◀ The 1980 Top 10 finishers list produced by IRONMAN.

1980 NAUTILUS TRIATHLON TOP TEN FINISHERS IN EACH EVENT

2.4 mile swim		112 mile bike race		26.2 mile marathon	
*DAVE SCOTT	.51	JOHN HOWARD	4.28	GORDON HALLER	3.27:15
THOMAS BOUGHEY	.55	*DAVE SCOTT	5.03	*DAVE SCOTT	3.30:33
RICK KOZLOWSKI	.55	JAMES MENSCHING	5.26	"BORN AGAIN SMITTY"	3.34:26
DAN SLOSBERG	.55	ERIC BINKER	5.33	LADDIE SHAW	3.34:42
RICHARD MERRITT	.59	DAVID CARLSON	5.34	GEORGE MUNRO	3.36:21
SAMUEL BARLOON	1.00	CHUCK NEUMANN	5.38	CHUCK NEUMANN	3.44:41
IAN EMBERSON	1.00	DEL SCHARFFENBERG	5.38	KENT DAVENPORT	3.45:16
KURT MADDEN	1.00	TOM WARREN	5.40	DAVID McGILLIVRAY	3.47:20
TOM WARREN	1.00	THOMAS BOUGHEY	5.43	HAL GABRIEL	3.49:39
CHUCK NEUMANN	1.02	DENNIS HEARST	5.43	**ROBIN BECK	3.56:24

*DAVE SCOTT - 1st MALE FINISHER

**ROBIN BECK - 1st FEMALE FINISHER

Collins was wrong: he was doubtful that the race could be as good to watch as it was to take part in. However, with the event televised, he was able to see his family's creation taken to a bigger – and very appreciative – audience when it aired in 1980 on the long-running series *Wide World of Sports*. By now, IRONMAN had more than a hundred men alongside two female participants and was popularizing the sport of triathlon all over the world. The audience watching at the time, however, did not see John Collins. He had been restationed by the Navy to a base in Washington, and had asked Nautilus if they would be interested in taking the IRONMAN race on.

Valerie Silk, of Nautilus, had mixed feelings about taking on the responsibility and initially turned Collins down. Her husband Hank convinced her otherwise, and a long-term involvement with the running and development of the IRONMAN business began. Despite her initial feelings, Valerie became instrumental in the event's evolution over the next decade. She later took on IRONMAN full-time while Hank focused on the Nautilus Fitness centers.

In many ways, IRONMAN remained a small operation. It was run from Silk's home with just two other staff members. Hawai'i was hours behind the mainland and her phone would ring at all hours of the day and night. But she grew to know almost all of the athletes – at a time when the numbers were manageable – and was able to appreciate their single-minded devotion to their sport. One man in the early days told her how he would get up early and train in the dark. He soon found that he was far from alone in that and, in IRONMAN, he had discovered his own community. Silk later said, "They were all like that to me. I was working my heart out for that. I wanted them all to have that experience." She would stand at the finish line and place leis around the necks of every finisher.

Immediately upon Nautilus taking over the running of the event, Silk made a number of important changes. One was to scrap the requirement that participants provide their own support crew. Another more visible change was to move the race to the Island of Hawai'i – the largest of the Hawaiian archipelago – for a date that was changed from February to October for the first time in 1982. The area around Kailua-Kona on Hawai'i became the focal point for the contest.

As the race grew in popularity, Silk wanted to avoid the attendant dangers of a congested race on O'ahu, a more densely populated area. An unexpected bonus of the move was that the heat, winds and black lava rock of the IRONMAN event's new home – although a greater challenge than the still shores of Waikiki – became an integral part of the race's appeal. Silk later recalled, "Once you've biked the Queen K [Queen Ka'ahumanu Highway, from Kailua-Kona to Hawi, on which participants are accompanied by blasts of the fearsome ho'o mumuku winds that reach up to 45mph] you've been to hell and back. That became part of the mystique." The October date also avoided winter storms and the rigors of transferring from a chilly new-year training program to the hotter climate of Kona.

First Annual
Hawaiian Iron Man
Triathlon
0700, 18 February 1978

Swim 2.4 miles!
Run 26¼ miles!
Bike 112 miles!
Brag the rest of your life!

late entries OK, but may have to wait for trophies.

Info from and Entries to
John F Collins
422 4544 (home)
474 5148 (work)
1656 Piikea St, Honolulu 96818

▲ The very first poster produced to promote the 1978 IRONMAN triathlon.

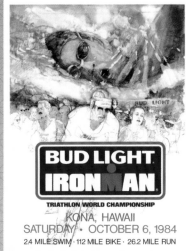

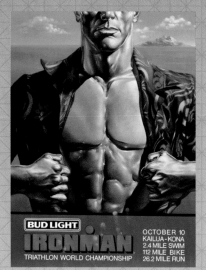

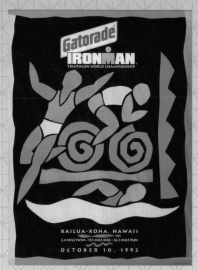

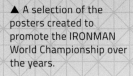

▲ A selection of the posters created to promote the IRONMAN World Championship over the years.

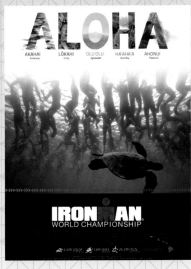

NAVY SEAL OF APPROVAL

▲ An afternoon view of Alli'i Drive without the athletes and spectators who line the road during the IRONMAN World Championship.

▶ Julie Moss, pictured on her way to winning a triathlon in 1984, whose efforts so entranced the watching audience in 1982.

Two years after taking over the race, Silk invited John Collins back to give his opinion on how the IRONMAN event had evolved. He was impressed with what he saw, telling Silk about his time as a naval engineer when he saw a ship cut in two before being pieced perfectly back together, down to the last piece of wiring. That feat was, in his view, on a similar level to what was being accomplished with IRONMAN. Silk was delighted. "Here was my hero," she said, "paying us such an incredible compliment."

The first IRONMAN race to take place in Kailua-Kona was won by John Howard in 9:38:29. Howard was a four-time Olympic cyclist who went on to set a cycling land speed record of 152.2mph in 1985, riding in the slipstream of a modified car on the salt flats of Utah. There were 20 female competitors in that first Island of Hawai'i race, led by Linda Sweeney,

who finished in 12:32. Another record set that day was by Walt Stack, who became the oldest competitor at age 70, finishing in 26:20:00. He would still be running when he turned 80, by which time he said he'd run more than 60,000 miles. For those watching on TV, it was clearer than ever that almost anyone had the potential to realize the IRONMAN athletes inside themselves – if they put the effort in. Fitness fans from all walks of life were beginning to understand that with proper training and a positive mind-set, finishing an IRONMAN race was an achievable goal.

Bud Light was sufficiently impressed with IRONMAN's growth to provide the first title sponsorship for the 1982 IRONMAN World Championship, underlining the progress that the brand was making. But it was an individual story that really propelled the event into popular consciousness.

Julie Moss, aged 23, entered the 1982 edition of the race as research for her exercise physiology thesis. She was not at that time what one might term a serious athlete, and she would later say, "I really wasn't ready for the pressure of leading the race." She had always dreaded being in the spotlight, whether in sport or at school, and as someone without any professional history, spectators could easily identify with her. By the end of the race, in the eyes of many of those spectators, Moss had come to embody the spirit of IRONMAN – without even winning. She had arrived in Hawai'i determined to enjoy the island and thought the atmosphere was terrific. Everything else – such as taking part in a tremendously demanding event, for example – was secondary. But as the big day arrived, her attitude began to change and she became more determined to win. She discovered her long-dormant competitive side, brought to life by the thrill of being in the race.

Yet, for a time, it seemed like Moss might take the IRONMAN title, at least until she started the last eight miles of the marathon. She had run a marathon six weeks before the IRONMAN race, and had experienced a similar feeling to what she was feeling now: exhaustion. As she approached the finish line, ABC's cameras captured an incredible story. She was forced to walk now and again over the closing miles, but always managed to get herself back running. Then, mere yards from the finish line, she staggered and fell to the ground. Kathleen McCartney, who was in second, passed her to take first place. In any normal race, that would have been the end of the story. But Moss was determined to cross the line.

"The image was that I was pretty out of it, but it was taking all my focus just to keep going," she later said. "I had to concentrate so much on how I placed my foot on the ground. If I was off by a bit, my leg would just buckle." She looked like a punch-drunk boxer as she repeatedly collapsed, got up, and carried on until she couldn't get up again. Unfortunately, widespread knowledge of race nutrition and hydration wasn't common at the time; her whole body was giving up on the race, and on her. By this point, she couldn't walk another step, much less run. She wasn't going to give up though, even if that meant crawling across the finish line. And that was exactly what she did.

With all eyes on Moss, Kathleen McCartney didn't even know she had taken first place until someone finally told her. But it was Moss's determination that would inspire those who followed her to live the IRONMAN mantra: "Anything is Possible." The next race saw hundreds more enter, having watched the images of Moss throw her arms over the finish line. She showed that the act of simply completing an IRONMAN race, rather than winning, was more than enough. Aspiring participants queued up for tickets and the race introduced a qualifying system to keep the field manageable. Competitors could now compete for a spot by racing an IRONMAN event in New Zeland, Japan, or Canada, where new races had been launched throughout the 1980s. Other changes in the fast-developing IRONMAN world included the introduction of cut-off times. Originally set at 18 hours and 30 minutes in 1982, the present-day cut-off time now stands at 17 hours. If an athlete is unable to finish in that time, they are not deemed a finisher.

The first mainland U.S. IRONMAN triathlon was held in Los Angeles in 1983, with top male and female finishers going on to Hawai`i in October. The winning woman was Canadian Sylviane Puntous, the first non-American to win the IRONMAN World Championship title. Or did she come in second? Spectators would be forgiven for seeing double, as the runner-up spot was taken by her identical twin Patricia, a

feat they repeated the following year. The pair enjoyed successful careers in triathlon events around the world.

Valerie Silk took on the chairmanship of the race in 1984, when she appointed Kona's Kay Rhead as race director. The Cold War was then at its height, but the global nature of IRONMAN was underlined when the first Eastern European athlete competed – Czechoslovakian Václav Vitovec. The IRONMAN series expanded internationally the following year, with qualifying races taking part in Auckland, New Zealand, in March and at Lake Biwa, Japan, in June.

The minimum age for participants had been set at 18 years old. The challenges of a full-blown IRONMAN event were an adult-only experience, with the rigors simply too much for growing bodies. However, there was a mounting desire for younger athletes to be able to experience a triathlon for the first time, which was why, in 1985, IRONKIDS® was born.

▲ An interview on the run: Olympic swimmer turned commentator Diana Nyad catches Jennifer Hinshaw on an uphill climb for a few words while she was leading the inaugural Los Angeles Ricoh IRONMAN triathlon in 1983.

CONTINUED EXPANSION

Younger athletes were able to take their first steps in the sport through IRONKIDS, an event started by the Sara Lee Corporation in 1985 as a way of promoting their bread. Children aged 7 to 14 could take part. A number of today's well-known athletes entered the first series of events as kids, including cyclist Lance Armstrong – runner-up in the first edition of the IRONKIDS event – Sara McLarty, and Olympic triathlete Hunter Kemper.

IRONMAN itself took on the IRONKIDS events in 2004. The focus of the youth races was far more on the fun of participation than on the competitive aspect. Just taking part in the events was, for the younger crowd, a way of learning more about the benefits and enjoyment of sport and of taking care of themselves with good nutrition and exercise. By 2018, more than 80 IRONKIDS events were held around the world, from Australia to the USA via Vietnam, UK, Germany, Poland and Bahrain.

Back in the world of IRONMAN, another step forward was taken in 1986 through the gift of an anonymous donor, who offered a fund of $100,000 prize money. It would seem obvious that Valerie Silk would jump at this opportunity, particularly as there had been no prize money on offer up until that point. But for her that had been part of the charm of the event – that it was strictly amateur. She did not want elite athletes, who may have felt that they had a right to more, to change the nature of the race. "When it appeared to me that these few people sort of felt a sense of entitlement, that got under my skin … my stubbornness got in the way," she later explained. She asked the advice of three other race directors, two of whom told her to take the money for the good of the growth of the sport. Fortunately, she took their advice.

The good fortune in 1986 did raise a further issue, however. The donor was only going to fund the prize money for one year. Silk was hesitant to make the commitment for future years, fearing that the money would have to come from other areas of the race. Funding the elite athletes at the very top of the sport might ultimately have a detrimental effect on the feeling of community that made the IRONMAN race so special.

As it turned out, the prizes did nothing to diminish the nature of the event. What's more, through the funds IRONMAN was able to increase its standing as an enlightened organization. From the very first financed race in 1986, men and women have enjoyed equal prize purses at IRONMAN events. It was one of the first professional sporting events anywhere in the world to apply this basic principle of equality.

The first prizes fittingly went to two of the greatest IRONMAN champions of all-time, Dave Scott and Paula Newby-Fraser of Zimbabwe, who finished in times of 8:28:37 and 9:49:14, respectively.

Ultimately, Silk remained the biggest fan of those who never had a hope of earning a penny. She said, "The really accomplished athlete gives us something we can admire and hope to achieve, but only in our dreams. The back-of-the-packers are the ones who are like most of us. And if they can do it, if they can actually cross the IRONMAN finish line, that gives us hope that it's within our grasp."

By this time, the race was attracting participants not only from all over the United States but across the globe. By 1987, 1,381 triathletes started the race, with 1,283 finishing within the time limit. The prize money on offer had increased to $150,000 and Dave Scott won the last of his six events with a time of 8:34:13. In a measure of how widespread the success of IRONMAN had become in the first decade of its existence, Kellogg's began calling its Pro Grain cereal "IRONMAN Food."

The first ten years of IRONMAN were celebrated by inviting the 15 men who first competed in 1978 back to race. Despite the repeat success of Paula Newby-Fraser, who came close to breaking the nine-hour mark (a feat she would go on to accomplish in 1992) and an exciting men's field eventually topped by Scott Molina, the 1988 IRONMAN race was marked with sadness over the death from cancer of race director Kay Rhead. She was succeeded by Debbie Baker.

▶ The champions of tomorrow! Ambitious young athletes test their mettle at an IRONKIDS event in Binz, Germany.

The 1989 race was to be the last under Valerie Silk's stewardship. As she moved on, she could look back on a decade with much to be proud of, but she said she reserved the greatest admiration for the IRONMAN volunteers. These dedicated individuals had grown from 900 people in 1980 – the first year that Silk ran the event – to around 3,500 by the time she stepped down. While that might seem like a large number, it's safe to say that they were all needed and very much appreciated by everyone involved, whether race official, athlete or supporter. By 2015, IRONMAN estimated that there were more than 650,000 items to be set up, put together, washed, cleaned, picked up, or disposed of by the time the last runners powered over the finish line. "I still, to this day, can't get over how much genuine deep love there was for the event by the volunteers," said Silk.

Throughout its history, IRONMAN had always focused on giving back to athletes and the community where each race is held. With a desire to do even more, the IRONMAN Foundation Inc. was launched in 2003 as a way to give back year-round by providing grant funding and service to local nonprofits within race communities.

Each year, the IRONMAN Foundation welcomes hundreds of athletes and volunteers to share in the mission of creating positive, tangible change by showing their service through sport and a commitment to community. Since 2003, over $50,000,000 has been provided through IRONMAN charitable giveback programs, including the IRONMAN Foundation, to more than 6,300 local, regional, national and global nonprofit initiatives.

Support for each IRONMAN race community is provided through multiple IRONMAN Foundation programs, giving athletes and volunteers the opportunity to customize their own IRONMAN experience through service.

The IRONMAN Foundation Community Fund works with local leaders to identify projects

◀ South African age group athlete Zoilie Mhlahlo refuels at the transition area during the 2017 IRONMAN African Championship in Port Elizabeth.

▼ One of the many volunteers – so beloved by Valerie Silk – who make IRONMAN events possible.

IRON WAR

It was the battle of the greats. If Julie Moss had defined what it meant to be an IRONMAN athlete, the 1989 race cemented the reputation of the event as being all about strength of character. Dave Scott and Mark Allen raced neck and neck for eight hours. After six previous attempts at the top spot, Allen finally overcame the dehydration, exhaustion and technical problems that had beset him in earlier years. He broke away from Scott with just two miles to go, winning in a record-smashing 8:09:15. Scott finished just 58 seconds later in 8:10:13 with the race's unofficial nickname, "Iron War," accurately summing up the titanic struggle. For the next few years, Allen was very much in the ascendant as an IRONMAN triathlete and would go on to match Scott's record (for a male athlete) of six titles.

► Dr James Gills celebrating at one of the many IRONMAN events he took part in over the years.

and provides grants to organizations of all sizes. From The Woods Project in Texas, who received $1,000 to support their life-changing outdoor programs for low-income students in Houston to All Hands Volunteers, who received $30,000 to build a community center in a relocation village for earthquake survivors in Manta, Ecuador, each grant is an opportunity to change the lives of people living in IRONMAN race communities.

Furthermore, the IRONMAN Foundation provides opportunities for hands-on giveback experiences through race week service projects, powerfully linking athletes with the local community. These projects range from large-scale Humanitarian Relief Efforts such as the Hurricane Maria rebuilding initiative in Puerto Rico, to building bikes for kids in need, to an adaptive surf clinic for youth with physical challenges in Oceanside, California.

Funding for the IRONMAN Foundation Community Fund is raised by athletes and includes the TEAM IMF program. TEAM IMF athletes are a catalyst for change. They pledge a minimum fundraising commitment for their race entries and share a unique opportunity to expand their journey to the finish line off

the course and into the community. Each year, the IRONMAN Foundation is represented by hundreds of athletes at races across the globe, including the IRONMAN World Championship.

Additional IRONMAN Foundation programming includes Women For Tri — created to break down barriers and increase female participation in triathlon by providing grant funding to local TriClubs — and the Humanitarian Relief Effort Campaign, which rallies the global IRONMAN community to support race communities recovering from natural disasters like Hurricanes Harvey, Irma and Maria and the Tubbs Wildfires in Santa Rosa, California.

Dr. James P. Gills, a veteran IRONMAN triathlete himself, took over as IRONMAN's owner in the early 1990s. Under the Gills family, World Triathlon Corporation (WTC) was established to oversee the growing number of IRONMAN events. From the new headquarters in Florida, the Gills were keen to preserve the essence of IRONMAN as a family-run business based on passion.

This was evident on a global scale as IRONMAN went on to flourish under the direction of some key stewards of its now-iconic brand – many of whom were inducted into the IRONMAN Hall of Fame over the years. After finishing the IRONMAN World Championship in 1985, one of IRONMAN's early pioneers, Canada's Graham Fraser, returned to organize his first triathlon in his hometown of Grimsby, Ontario. Within a decade, his race had grown into a series which, at the time, was the largest in the world. In 1996, Fraser took over the decade-old IRONMAN Canada in Penticton, British Columbia, the third full-distance race in the global circuit that at the time included the IRONMAN World Championship, IRONMAN New Zealand, and IRONMAN Japan. As a response to incredible demand, Fraser went on to lead the expansion of IRONMAN racing across North America, adding six full-distance races to the North American calendar, including Lake Placid and Florida.

Across the pond, Austrian trio Georg Hochegger, Stefan Petschnig, and Helge Lorenz created a company in 1997 called Triangle Events with the goal of launching an IRONMAN event in their hometown of Klagenfurt. Triangle Events would go on to create licensed full-distance events in France and South Africa, along with IRONMAN 70.3 races in Monaco, South Africa, and a second Austrian event in St. Pölten. The trio was instrumental in establishing a solid foundation of well-run races that has contributed to the existing popularity of IRONMAN races in the region today.

The successes of these two entities were buoyed by Lew Friedland, who, after working with IRONMAN in various capacities, took over as president from 1998 until 2004. Friedland had been captivated by IRONMAN at the IRONMAN World Championship in 1989 while watching the "Iron War" between Mark Allen and Dave Scott. By working with the company's first licensees and event producers such as Fraser and Triangle, Friedland was at the helm of the company's growth during the era. He helped launch historic and well-loved events such as IRONMAN Coeur d'Alene, IRONMAN Arizona, and IRONMAN 70.3 Oceanside, in addition to key races in South Africa, the United Kingdom, France, Malaysia, and Korea.

It wasn't just business expansion, however, that gave IRONMAN its heart and soul through the first decade. Others worked behind the scenes and on its front lines, including 1988 IRONMAN World Championship finisher, Dr. Bob Laird, the man responsible for developing medical protocols for the marquee event. The man known to most simply as "Dr. Bob" has helped improve the medical care IRONMAN triathletes receive around the world.

Another is San Diego race announcer Mike Reilly, who coined the mantra athletes all over the world now crave to hear when they cross the finish line: "You Are an IRONMAN." The year was 1991 – Reilly's third year calling athletes across the most famous finish line in the sport. A friend of Reilly's from San Diego, Dan Trone, was competing, and had expressed to Reilly just days before the race that he was concerned about how he would do. Reilly assured him that when it came to it, Trone would indeed be an IRONMAN. On race day, when Reilly saw Trone

IRONMAN HALL OF FAME

The IRONMAN Hall of Fame was founded in 1993 to honor those who make outstanding contributions to the growth of IRONMAN. Some inductees have been athletes, some have set records, and others have been instrumental in running IRONMAN and taking it to new heights.

1993 Dave Scott
1994 Julie Moss
1995 Scott Tinley
1996 Paula Newby-Fraser
1997 Mark Allen
1998 John and Judy Collins
1999 Valerie Silk
2000 Tom Warren
2001 Dr. Bob Laird
2002 Bob Babbitt
2003 John MacLean, Gordon Haller, Lyn Lemaire
2004 Greg Welch
2005 Jim MacLaren
2008 Rick and Dick Hoyt ("Team Hoyt")
2011 Mike Reilly
2012 Graham Fraser
2013 Peter Henning
2014 Georg Hochegger, Helge Lorenz, Stefan Petschnig
2015 Lori Bowden, Heather Fuhr
2016 Lew Friedland, Peter Reid
2017 Chrissie Wellington
2018 Erin Baker, Scott Molina, Ken Baggs, Rocky Campbell

Henning's 12 years with the company. Henning and his crew subsequently introduced the world to many inspiring IRONMAN athletes, including Jon "Blazeman" Blais, who completed the race in Kona with ALS; Sister Madonna Buder, then the oldest female IRONMAN finisher; and the handcycle battle between Carlos Moleda and David Bailey. The 2013 IRONMAN Hall of Fame inductee helped the coverage of the IRONMAN World Championship win its 16th Emmy in 2012 for Outstanding Camera Work. (It won a 17th in 2018.) By 2017, IRONMAN was watched by more than 4.7 million viewers worldwide, who were collectively taking in more than 33 million minutes of live coverage. The largest audience in 2017 remained within the United States, followed by Brazil, Spain, Germany, and the UK.

In 1992, there was much for the TV audience to watch and admire. Three-time defending champion Mark Allen was one of four men to break the cycling record before the race became another Iron War-style duel between Allen and Cristián Bustos of Chile during the marathon. Allen eventually broke away to become the first person to win four consecutive titles, setting a record time of 8:09:08 in the process. There was more drama to come as Paula Newby-Fraser made good on her early promise and did what everyone involved in triathlon had thought she might be the one to do — becoming the first woman to break the nine-hour barrier at the full distance, finishing in 8:55:28.

Physical challenges have not been a barrier to taking part in IRONMAN races. There are now two different divisions who compete in IRONMAN events: Physically Challenged (PC) athletes and Handcycle (HC) athletes. The PC division is available to those with either a visual impairment or a physical or neurological impairment that substantially limits one or more major life activity. Before these divisions had been formally established at every IRONMAN event, there were a number of stand-out competitors who were inspirations to all of those who came after them. Early PC athletes include the race's first deaf competitor, Michael Russo, who competed in 1984, and Jim MacLaren, a former American football player from the east coast of the U.S. who lost the lower part of his left leg in a motorcycle accident. He completed the 1991 World Championship cycling and running with a custom-designed prosthesis that quickly caught the attention of the crowd.

▲ The first IRONMAN Hall of Famer: Dave Scott smiles as he breaks the tape in a record time at the 1982 IRONMAN World Championship.

coming down the finish chute, he exuberantly strung together a phrase he'd go on to say hundreds of thousands of times more: "Dan Trone, YOU are an IRONMAN!" Reilly eventually came to be known as the "Voice of IRONMAN" and was inducted into the IRONMAN Hall of Fame in 2011.

During this era, WTC also took over all aspects of the broadcast of the IRONMAN World Championship and made it a standalone program in its own right rather than a part of a general sports show. IRONMAN moved the broadcast to NBC, another major US network, and the program went on to receive a total of more than 50 Emmy Award nominations under Peter

The first HC athlete was Dr. Jon Franks, a paraplegic athlete from California, who in 1994 asked to use a hand-cycle for the cycling and a racing wheelchair for the marathon. In the end, Franks just missed the cut-off time and did not finish but, like predecessor Julie Moss, he was a great inspiration to all of the IRONMAN spectators watching. In particular, he had showed incredible determination in climbing the last hill of the bike course, and as a result, many other physically challenged sports fans realized they could do it too.

After Franks's example, a number of other HC athletes came forward to take on the challenge of competing in and finishing an IRONMAN event. In 1996, John MacLean of Australia was the first to complete the event as an HC athlete within the overall time of 17 hours, and in 1997 he became the first athlete using a hand-cranked bicycle and wheelchair to finish the event within the cut-off times for each discipline. That same year, WTC's years of planning and careful research led to the establishment of both formal HC and PC categories available to be competed in at various races.

In that first event, eight participants competed as PC athletes. Clarinda Brueck

▼ Minda Dentler is one of many HC athletes who have thrived in IRONMAN competitions since Dr. John Franks first raced in his wheelchair and hand-cycle.

▲ A large group of colorful spectators gather to encourage athletes competing in the 2016 IRONMAN Wales in Pembroke, Wales.

from New Jersey was the first female to finish; she was born without the lower portion of her left arm but still triumphed over many of the able-bodied entrants. For her, as much as for any IRONMAN athlete, competing was an empowering experience that would inspire others who might not have dreamed of taking part before seeing her efforts. Later, Jon Blais became the first athlete with amyotrophic lateral sclerosis (ALS) to finish the race, log-rolling across the finish line in 2005 in what he said was a symbol of his fight against the condition. "Even if I have to be rolled across the finish line," he declared, "I'm finishing." Blais, who died of the illness in 2007, couldn't know then that his actions, which would later become known as the "Blazeman roll", would go on to become a staple at IRONMAN finish lines all over the world in support of the battle against motor neuron diseases of all kinds.

Full HC and PC divisions were officially established at the first IRONMAN World Championship in the year following Blais's appearance. The two divisions each have their own rules for entry and for competition, and there was subsequently a notable increase in interest from PC and HC athletes alike.

HC athletes can now take part in any of three annual qualifying events held around the world that allow them to qualify to race at the IRONMAN World Championship. PC competitors do not have qualifying slots for the World Championship – instead, IRONMAN completes a drawing for PC athletes who want to take part and have finshed an IRONMAN or IRONMAN 70.3 event during the previous year.

John Collins returned in 1998 to help celebrate IRONMAN's 20th anniversary. He made it across the finish line in 16:30:02, which was especially impressive considering he was an athlete who had taken a 19-year break from IRONMAN competitions. In all, seven of the original 15 competitors from 1978 were on hand to watch the race, while six of them competed. Among them was the inaugural IRONMAN winner Gordon Haller, who finished in 14:27:01. A further 17 of the 21 past champions finished on the day, including Scott Molina, Heather Fuhr

Paula Newby-Fraser, Tom Warren and the then course record-holder Luc Van Lierde.

Enthusiasm was at an all-time high as IRONMAN entered its third decade. The first person to finish 20 consecutive IRONMAN World Championship races took to the field in 1999 – Lyn Brooks, then 51, finished in 14:44:20. During that same race, Scott Tinley announced his retirement after 20 appearances in the competition. As the turn of the millennium approached, the Internet was at the peak of its first boom. Every opportunity to increase global awareness of IRONMAN was taken, and the 2000 IRONMAN World Championship was streamed for the first time on ironman.com. The live streaming was a success; a few years later, organizers made their first foray onto eBay, auctioning off 20 entry spots and raising more than $400,000.

IRONMAN was now well established across the globe, with new races in South Africa, Asia, Korea, and Malaysia, as well as closer to home in California. With growth came the opportunity to experiment with new race formats, such

as an event featuring half the distances of IRONMAN – still a phenomenal challenge. What later became the IRONMAN 70.3® series (the number a reference to the total number of miles in the event – 1.2-mile swim, 56-mile bike ride and 13.1-mile half-marathon) began as Half IRONMAN UK in Llanberis. The little village is situated in Wales at the foot of Snowdon, the country's highest mountain and a magnet for climbers, walkers, and runners. Llanberis hosted the event for two years before it moved to Sherborne and then Longleat in the UK, where it became the first event to take the IRONMAN 70.3 name.

The IRONMAN 70.3 series now boasts more than 110 events around the world and has its own World Championship. The first of these was held in 2006 in Clearwater, Florida, and it was here that Australian Craig "Crowie" Alexander and Canadian Samantha McGlone won in 3:45:37 and 4:12:58, respectively. In 2011, Crowie became the first person ever to win both the IRONMAN 70.3 and IRONMAN World Championship titles in the same year –

▲ A professional athlete competes in the bike portion of the IRONMAN African Championship, South Africa.

"I was able to handle racing in extreme heat, so when it got hot, or even better, when it became hot and humid, I was thankful to be warm and not freezing. I was good at coping with the extreme conditions in Hawai'i, rather than let those conditions beat me."

LORI BOWDEN, TWO-TIME IRONMAN WORLD CHAMPION AND HALL OF FAME INDUCTEE

in the process, he notched his third IRONMAN World Championship.

By the time of his latest victory, the IRONMAN 70.3 World Championship was being staged a month before the big event in Hawai`i, which meant the half-distance could be used as a final testing ground in training for those who had made it on the list for the Kona starting line.

IRONMAN was in an excellent position when it celebrated its 25th anniversary in 2003. The TV coverage moved to a coveted primetime slot and viewers were able to see Canadians Peter Reid and Lori Bowden come in at 8:22:35 and 9:11:55, respectively. Both were former World Champions and Reid had won a total of 10 IRONMAN triathlons, marking his final Kona victory in 2003. Bowden, meanwhile, was a dominating force in the IRONMAN world of the late 1990s and early 2000s and explained of her passion, "I have always loved racing in Hawai`i. It always seemed so hard to qualify for Kona that I always felt extremely fortunate and grateful to be able to go there and be a part of it. I loved the whole experience there, nerves and all."

In 2008, the year of the 30th anniversary, 1,636 athletes – men and women from all over the world an ranging in age from 18 to 79 – crossed the finish line in Kona. This IRONMAN World Championship saw the first win for Australian Craig Alexander, while Chrissie Wellington took home her second title, having been the first British athlete to win the title the previous year. An impressive 30th anniversary line-up in the men's field included

former IRONMAN World Champions such as Chris McCormack, Normann Stadler and Faris Al-Sultan, among other top contenders such as Chris Lieto, Eneko Llanos, and Rutger Beke.

In many ways, IRONMAN came of age in its fourth decade, when the brand expanded dramatically—first under Providence Equity, who hired current CEO Andrew Messick in 2011—and then under the Chinese Dalian Wanda group, who bought WTC in 2015.

Andrew Messick realized that IRONMAN was more than just a race brand. Not only was each individual race a platform for finishers to realize their greatness and test the limits of their potential, but also the increasing number of finishers was creating a global community of athletes.

These athletes, whether amateur or professional, were no longer happy to treat IRONMAN races as a one-and-done affair; something to be ticked off of the bucket list before moving on to the next challenge. Instead, athletes were increasingly looking to the next race and the next challenge. As a multiple-IRONMAN finisher himself, Messick understood this desire completely and set about nurturing this community, setting up IRONMAN events in many new countries, some of which had never held a major triathlon event before.

There are now over 40 IRONMAN races, 110 IRONMAN 70.3 races and a number of other short-course triathlons and multi-sport events run by IRONMAN – with new events developing on a regular basis. These events occur in 55

different countries spread across six continents, and more than one million athletes register for them each year.

What is more, while the IRONMAN World Championship still maintains its prestige as the ultimate goal of IRONMAN athletes, numerous regional championships were developed that take place annually on each of the different continents and provide qualifying spots for the IRONMAN World Championship. These regional championships take place in both the IRONMAN and the IRONMAN 70.3 formats.

With so many more races taking place around the world, and in the spirit of the IRONMAN global community, a system was needed to allow athletes in events taking place in, say, Bahrain, Australia or Sri Lanka to compare themselves with athletes racing in the

◤ The new 2018 co-branded IRONMAN/Ventum bike collection.

U.S., Germany or Argentina, which may have very different racing conditions.

In order to track and compare athletes' performances across all of the races, the IRONMAN All World Athlete Program was created in 2015. Athletes who finished in the top 10 percent of their age groups in both IRONMAN 70.3 and IRONMAN could now use their top three race finishes towards earning a bronze, silver, or gold designation (for those ending up in the 1st, 5th,and 10th percent, respectively.)

In 2014, the IRONMAN 70.3 World Championship began a new annual global rotation with a race in Mont-Tremblant, Quebec, Canada. In 2015, it was held in Europe for the first time, and in 2016 on the Sunshine Coast,

Australia. In 2017, the event switched to a two-day format, featuring the women's race on Saturday followed by the men's race on Sunday, in Chattanooga, Tennessee. This format has continued in Port Elizabeth, South Africa, in 2018 and in Nice, France, in 2019.

IRONMAN's global reach was further underlined when their partnership with the International Triathlon Union (ITU) was announced in early 2017. The goal was to further develop and standardize the sport and ensure its fairness. It was an indication not only of how far IRONMAN had come, but also how its core values remained constant since that first race back in 1978. For John Collins and his family, IRONMAN had been about participation while establishing fantastic new targets, and

▶ An athlete runs towards his bike in the transition area at the 2015 IRONMAN Austria-Kärnten.

▼ Female athletes line up at the start of the 2017 IRONMAN 70.3 World Championship in Chattanooga, Tennessee.

trying to reach them. Forty years later, there might be more than 2,400 competitors starting at Kona, but the same core values and beliefs hold true for all of them.

In recent years, IRONMAN has expanded beyond triathlon, purchasing and developing running, cycling and mountain biking events all around the world, with the four separate event types now making up the four pillars of the IRONMAN family, and making it the leading mass-participation sports company in the world.

Messick treated IRONMAN as a global brand and invested resources to ensure that the athlete experience was uniformly superb. As a multiple IRONMAN finisher, Messick understood that exceptional operational delivery was a fundamental requirement for IRONMAN's long-term success. Messick introduced a rigorous benchmarking and organizational building process to ensure that the delivery of the athlete experience was world class.

It was clear to IRONMAN's leadership team that the race that had grown up in Hawai`i had captured the imaginations of the world's passionate and aspiring athletes alike. Under Messick, IRONMAN began a program of improving the quality of its events, expanding globally by creating new races around the world, rotating the IRONMAN 70.3 World Championship, and creating a stronger and more vibrant global athlete community.

IRONMAN says, "Anything Is Possible." Countless IRONMAN competitors have proven over the years that when it comes to triathlon races – even over what, for most ordinary sports participants, seems like an unimaginable distance – that is entirely true. While it might be necessary to trudge, limp, crawl or roll over the IRONMAN finish line, with the right mindset and training, there is always the possibility of competing in and finishing one of the many IRONMAN races available all around the world – and perhaps even qualifying for the IRONMAN World Championship in Kailua-Kona, Hawai`i.

What's more, it is never too late to begin the journey to the IRONMAN World Championship. In 2016, Hiromu Inada became the oldest competitor to finish at Kona in a time of 16:49:13 at the awe-inspiring age of 83 years old. He overtook Sister Madonna Buder, a Roman Catholic sister known as the "Iron Nun," as the oldest IRONMAN finisher; she remains the oldest woman to finish, though, having

completed IRONMAN Canada at the age of 82 in 2012. It is competitors such as these who provide inspiration for the next generation of IRONMAN triathletes.

What binds athletes together across the diverse portfolio of events IRONMAN now organizes is that every competitor is challenged and inspired every step of the way. Each one of them – triathlete, swimmer, cyclist, or runner – is part of the global community of men and women striving to push themselves and one other to new possibilities.

▲ The Iron Nun – Sister Madonna Buder – begins the bike leg of the 2007 IRONMAN World Championship.

◄ "The Voice of IRONMAN": legendary race announcer Mike Reilly at work encouraging athletes to the finish line at IRONMAN Boulder in 2014.

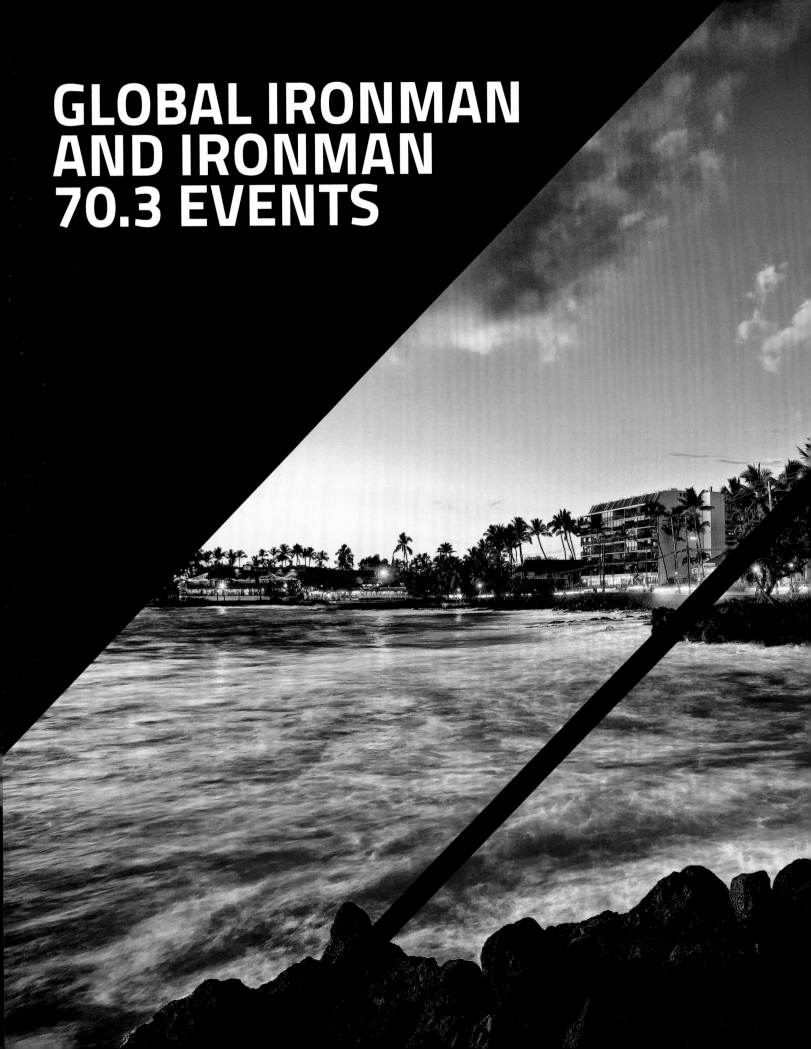

GLOBAL IRONMAN AND IRONMAN 70.3 EVENTS

There is more to IRONMAN® events than just the legendary IRONMAN World Championship in Kailua-Kona, Hawai`i. No matter where an athlete might live or hope to travel to, they will never be too far from an IRONMAN or IRONMAN 70.3® event. All of these races offer not just the thrill of taking part and competing in a well-planned and spectacularly scenic event, but many also include the possibility of earning an automatic slot to the IRONMAN World Championship or the IRONMAN 70.3 World Championship. These slots are allocated to the winners of each age group for both male and female athletes in each event. When there are more qualifying slots than age groups running, the remaining slots are divided up among the groups in proportion to how many runners there are in each category, so athletes need not necessarily win their group to book a place at Kona.

◄ A sunset over Ali'i Drive on Kailua-Kona.

REGIONAL IRONMAN CHAMPIONSHIPS

STANDARD BANK IRONMAN AFRICAN CHAMPIONSHIP SOUTH AFRICA
Nelson Mandela Bay, South Africa
Qualifying Slots (QS): 80 for the same-year IRONMAN World Championship

▼ The IRONMAN African Championship South Africa boasts one of the most spectacular cycle courses in the world as athletes bike the southern coast of South Africa.

There has been an annual IRONMAN race in Nelson Mandela Bay for more than a decade, but the venue was busier than usual in 2018. It played host to the IRONMAN 70.3 World Championship, which rotates globally each year. The setting remained the same – Port Elizabeth, South Africa's second oldest city – a quiet beachside town by comparison to Johannesburg and Cape Town – and one of the country's three capital cities. The day

begins with a one-lap swim course beginning on Hobie Beach, athletes setting out parallel from the pier. The course then goes past Humewood Beach all the way to Kings Beach before turning and heading back. The water temperature is usually around 70°F and the conditions are generally calm.

The bike course takes athletes out on two flat, fast laps with sweeping views of the ocean and the rugged coastline of a marine-protected area, before moving slightly inland for the undulating countryside section. The return brings competitors along the coast to the transition area to start the run. Here there will be no shortage of support from the crowd, with more than 80,000 friends, family and fans on hand to cheer the runners to the final finish line along Marine Drive.

MEMORIAL HERMANN IRONMAN NORTH AMERICAN CHAMPIONSHIP TEXAS

The Woodlands, Texas, USA

QS: 80 for the same-year IRONMAN World Championship

With a population of around 100,000, The Woodlands is a new city in Texas, established only in the early 1970s and situated some 27 miles north of Houston. It is pedestrian-friendly, easy to navigate, and has been voted among the Top 10 in IRONMAN's athlete survey for best "Run Course," "Host City Experience," and "Post-Race Celebration." The race itself is welcoming to new competitors, providing specific support for newcomers to the event, and there is an IRONMAN Village to serve as the hub of activities. If that isn't a big enough draw, the spring event offers the joint-most qualifying slots to the IRONMAN World Championship of any full-distance events.

Athletes begin with a 2.4-mile rolling-start point-to-point swim in Lake Woodlands, beginning at North Shore Park and ending at Town Green Park. A two-loop out-and-back 112-mile bike course takes participants south through the scenic, rolling farmland of east Texas, the majority of which is closed to traffic and is fast and flat. The day ends with a 26.2-mile run, taking place entirely within The Woodlands and concluding with a spectacular finish on Waterway Avenue.

▲ The run course of the IRONMAN North American Championship Texas circles Lake Woodlands.

CAIRNS AIRPORT IRONMAN ASIA-PACIFIC CHAMPIONSHIP CAIRNS
Cairns, Queensland, Australia
QS: 80 for the same-year IRONMAN World Championship

Situated at the gateway to the Great Barrier Reef, this IRONMAN event has a stunning backdrop for competitors to do battle against, including the UNESCO World Heritage-listed Daintree National Park rainforest and the beauty of a tropical island. In 2018, the event was part of the Cairns Airport Adventure Festival, which included the IRONMAN 70.3 race as well as an IRONKIDS® race among its attractions. Cairns celebrated seven years of IRONMAN races in 2018 and participants have voted the event among the Top 10 in IRONMAN's survey in the best "Overall Bike" element as well as "Best Music."

The swim begins from a beach in the Coral Sea where the tropical temperatures ensure an enjoyably balmy dip with water temperatures normally around 75°F. The bike course races up the Captain Cook Highway on the coastline from Cairns to Port Douglas and finishes in the heart of the city where great crowd support can be appreciated by the athletes; it is particularly strong in the final stages of the run, which can be very helpful for tiring competitors.

▲ From reef to rainforest, via coastal cliff, the IRONMAN Asia-Pacific Championship in Cairns, Australia, offers incredible views throughout the day.

MAINOVA IRONMAN EUROPEAN CHAMPIONSHIP FRANKFURT

Frankfurt, Germany

QS: 80 for the same-year IRONMAN World Championship

The Frankfurt bike section is one of the best supported on the entire race circuit, with a picturesque finish in the heart of the old city. Those who have enough energy to explore beyond the course of the race can visit the Frankfurt Zoological Garden, the Goethe Museum, and the old opera house among other attractions in close proximity to the event.

Athletes begin the race with a swim in the quiet waters of the Langener Waldsee Lake. The two-loop course has a short run between the laps. The water temperature is usually between 71°F and 75°F. The two-loop cycle course guides athletes through the middle of Frankfurt

▼ The calm waters of the Langener Waldsee await the athletes at start of the IRONMAN European Championship in Frankfurt.

▶ The bike course passes through Frankfurt. Roads are closed to traffic, but not to the thousands of spectators who come out.

and into surrounding small villages. The route, which is closed to traffic, is hilly and challenging, mixed with some easier flat sections. The flat-run course consists of four fast laps, which provide the best possible scenario for ambitious athletes to reach their best marathon times. The run is also fully stocked with amazingly supportive fans, who gather to cheer wildly along the promenade next to the river.

There are a number of events scheduled around the IRONMAN race. A few days beforehand, IRONKIDS athletes compete in their event while collecting money for a good cause by running laps in the Mainkai Arena. Later on is the NightRun, a 5K relay run for amateur athletes.

IRONMAN SOUTH AMERICAN CHAMPIONSHIP
Mar del Plata, Argentina
QS: 75 for the following-year IRONMAN World Championship

The Argentine IRONMAN event is a new addition to the family of races, having first been staged in 2017. It has quickly become a favorite among athletes, coming in the Top 10 in IRONMAN's survey of competitors for "Will Attend Next Year" and "Overall Bike" categories. And after just one race, it was designated as the venue for the South American Championship.

Mar del Plata is on the coast in eastern Argentina, in the Buenos Aires province, south of the capital itself. It features beaches and promenades alongside the Atlantic Ocean, with the sea providing a theme for the race as a whole; the two loops of the swim are held in the ocean. Competitors keep the shimmering waters in view for most of the cycling course, which runs along a coastal road before doubling back and only heading inland relatively briefly. The last stage of the race is made up of a run of three laps that once again hugs the shoreline on a course that is flat and not short of enthusiastic support. Athletes are greeted at the finish line by the welcoming sight of one of the symbols of the town: a large gold statue of a sea lion.

▲ The coast of Mar del Plata provides a sensational venue for the IRONMAN South American Championship.

REGIONAL IRONMAN 70.3 CHAMPIONSHIPS

IRONMAN 70.3 SOUTH AMERICAN CHAMPIONSHIP

Buenos Aires, Argentina

QS: 75 for the following-year IRONMAN 70.3 World Championship

Dedicated competitors in South America have no shortage of locations to test their mettle, including IRONMAN and IRONMAN 70.3 events in Brazil, Chile, Colombia, Costa Rica, Ecuador, Peru, Uruguay, and no fewer than three races in Argentina alone. Alongside the IRONMAN South American Championship in Mar del Plata, there is an IRONMAN 70.3 race held in Bariloche and the chance for racers to take in the splendor of the Argentine capital itself – Buenos Aires.

A recent addition to the circuit, Buenos Aires offers a temperate climate for athletes to test out their ability, with temperatures usually between 75°F and 89°F. The event itself takes place about 25 minutes away from the heart of Buenos Aires and is an easy journey from the airport. The swim begins in a small, calm lake before heading through transition and on to the bike, where there is the opportunity for a good time with a fast and flat course. The course finishes with the run, where participants have just one lap with plenty of space for spectators to show their support. As the best-attended race for this distance, the race was among the Top 10 in IRONMAN's survey for the "Will Attend Next Year" category in 2017.

▼ The IRONMAN 70.3 South American Championship course centers around the warm waters of the Puerto Canoas, where spectators flock to watch the race.

IRONMAN 70.3 NORTH AMERICAN PRO CHAMPIONSHIP ST. GEORGE
Utah, USA
QS: 75 for the same-year IRONMAN 70.3 World Championship

The St. George event occurs against the stunning backdrop of the distinctive red rock sandstone mountains of southern Utah. It is also one of the toughest and most scenic races on the circuit, which gives it a certain caché among athletes. It attracts top professional athletes and the town comes out en masse to cheer on the competitors.

Even the most dedicated athlete should pause for a moment to take in the scenery at the Sand Hollow State Park before plunging into the one-loop swim course in the blue waters of the reservoir, where the water temperature is around 60°F. The cycle leg of the race begins by carving through the rolling hills of the Sand Hollow Reservoir before taking the field through St. George and into the city of Ivins along a flat, fast section. It finishes by climbing up and through Snow Canyon State Park. As a reward for the ascent, there are extraordinary views that combine well with the knowledge that it is now downhill all the way back to St. George. More amazing vistas can be observed as the run takes competitors through the Red Cliffs Desert Reserve, where the city is laid out below them. The finish line is in the center of St. George itself, located on Main Street.

▶ The stunning red rocks of Utah provide the backdrop for the hilly course at the IRONMAN 70.3 St. George.

KMD IRONMAN 70.3 EUROPEAN CHAMPIONSHIP ELSINORE

Elsinore, Denmark

QS: 75 for the same-year IRONMAN 70.3 World Championship

"To race in Elsinore or not to race in Elsinore? That is the question. Whether 'tis nobler in the mind to suffer the slings and arrows of outrageous running schedules..." Okay, that's enough *Hamlet*. The setting for Shakespeare's masterpiece is also the home of a popular IRONMAN 70.3 event in Europe, situated in northern Denmark, just a few miles across the strait from Sweden.

Following the event's opening ceremony, there are enough sporting theatrics to keep any fan happy, including a swim in the harbor in the old ferry terminal and a countryside cycle course. Cyclists take in the north Zeeland coastline in one loop before leaping off the bike for a run around the city center itself, under the watchful gaze of Kronborg Castle, a UNESCO World Heritage site and the heart of the bard's masterpiece. Elsinore, known in Danish as Helsingør, is also home to an IRONKIDS event in the form of a run that takes place on the same day.

There are other events in Denmark that take place throughout the year. IRONMAN holds the KMD 5150™ race and an IRONKIDS event in Aarhus. Additionally, there is a weekend in the country's capital city, Copenhagen, which combines both IRONMAN and IRONKIDS events.

▲ The world-famous Kronborg Castle, immortalized as Elsinore in *Hamlet*, overlooks the majority of the run course at the IRONMAN 70.3 Elsinore in Denmark.

REGENT AGUILA IRONMAN 70.3 ASIA-PACIFIC CHAMPIONSHIP

Cebu, Philippines

QS: 50 for the next-year IRONMAN 70.3 World Championship

◄ Canada's Brent McMahon on his way to victory in a time of 3:59:05 at the 2014 IRONMAN 70.3 in Cebu.

Cebu – one of the most desirable island destinations in the Asian-Pacific – has hosted the IRONMAN 70.3 in the Philippines since 2012. Conditions can make this a tough event for athletes; temperatures of 90°F and higher are to be expected, as are the famous Cebu head- and crosswinds. However, the race is as beautiful as it is challenging.

The race centers around the aptly named Shangri-La Mactan Resort and Spa, which is set amongst a lush tropical landscape and its own spectacular private beach cove, and boasts a multitude of activities to do both before and after the race. The swim course begins and ends at the beach of the resort, with the swim taking place in the crystal-clear azure waters of the sea. The notoriously windy bike course shows off the best the tropical island has to offer, as the route forms a loop traversing four cities while rarely leaving the stunning coastline. The race finishes with a run course looping from the Shangri-La Mactan Resort to the very tip of the island and back again.

IRONMAN 70.3 MIDDLE EAST CHAMPIONSHIP

Manama, Bahrain

QS: 75 for the following-year IRONMAN 70.3 World Championship, 10 military slots for the following-year IRONMAN World Championship

▲ Children compete in the IRONKIDS event preceding the IRONMAN 70.3 Middle East Championship in Bahrain.

◄ A cyclist passes under the watchful eye of the Al Fateh Grand Mosque in Bahrain, one of a number of impressive landmarks around the course.

Bahrain forms a unique backdrop for a race for many athletes visiting from other parts of the world. Organizers promise an insight into local culture over the weekend of the event against the dramatic backdrop of the northern city of Manama. The festive opening and closing ceremonies will delight both athletes and their supporters.

The headline event begins off the waters of the iconic H-shaped Four Seasons Hotel, which looms over the coast at over 650 feet in height – the fourth-highest structure in all of Bahrain. This sets the scene for a spectacular course with a single transition and countless supporters along the way. The flat and fast bike course is a single loop that includes iconic buildings and attractions such as the Bahrain World Trade Centre (standing even taller than the Four Seasons at 787 feet) and a rather special lap on the home course of the country's Formula One Grand Prix race. Manama's run element takes place in Bahrain Bay itself, a course voted in the Top 10 best "Overall Run" in IRONMAN's survey – impressive for a race that only began in 2015.

OTHER POPULAR IRONMAN EVENTS

IRONMAN MARYLAND
Cambridge, Maryland, USA
QS: 40 for the next-year IRONMAN World Championship

Winner of numerous "Athletes' Choice" awards, this fall race begins with a 2.4-mile swim in the fresh water of the Choptank River on the Delmarva Peninsula. The 112-mile flat, fast and scenic bike course takes athletes through Dorchester County and into the Blackwater National Wildlife Reserve – a critical waterfowl sanctuary for birds migrating along the Atlantic Flyway and containing nearly one-third of Maryland's tidal wetlands. The refuge is home to over 250 bird species, 35 species of reptiles and amphibians, 165 species of threatened and endangered plants, and numerous mammals that can be spotted throughout the year in the region's marshes, forests, meadows, and fields. The day finishes with a 26.2-mile run on country roads offering numerous straightaways, and ends in the heart of historic Cambridge, Massachusetts.

SUBARU IRONMAN CANADA
Whistler, British Columbia, Canada
QS: 40 for the same-year IRONMAN World Championship

IRONMAN Canada builds on the tradition of the namesake race that has been part of the IRONMAN circuit for over 30 years. Since moving to the mountain ski resort town of Whistler in 2013, it has wowed athletes and supporters year after year. The race runs through the traditional territory of the Squamish & Lil'wat Nations. The two-loop, 2.4-mile swim takes place in the clean, shallow waters of Alta Lake. Athletes transition to their bikes at a lakeside transition area before beginning a challenging and scenic 112-mile bike course that traverses the Sea to Sky Highway and Callaghan Valley (the site of the Nordic skiing events during the 2010 Winter Olympics). The run course follows the meandering Valley Trail past Lost Lake and Green Lake, allowing spectators plenty of opportunities to cheer for their athletes. The day ends in Whistler's Olympic Plaza, a central and festive location to celebrate and begin a week in one of the most visitor-friendly regions of Western Canada.

▲ The IRONMAN Maryland course runs through the beautiful Blackwater National Wildlife Reserve, providing plenty of scenic views for the athletes.

▼ American Linsey Corbin bikes through the forest in the 2017 IRONMAN Canada.

KELLOGG'S NUTRI-GRAIN IRONMAN NEW ZEALAND

Taupo, New Zealand

QS: 40 for the next-year IRONMAN World Championship

With half the field coming from outside the country every year, IRONMAN New Zealand is truly the world's most international IRONMAN. This race has stood the test of time and will celebrate 35 incredible years in 2019. Firmly established in its hometown of Taupo since 1999, the event showcases the best New Zealand and its breath-taking scenery has to offer. Thanks to the locals' pure Kiwi spirit, athletes feel like they belong the minute they arrive. The event attracts more than 2,000 volunteers from a population of just 22,000 – and athletes will encounter the rest along the streets cheering them on. One of the world's biggest fresh water lakes offers arguably the best swim on the circuit. A two-loop bike course comes back through town before heading through the forests, and a three-loop run course leaves athletes no chance to escape the thousands of spectators. Kellogg's Nutri-Grain IRONMAN New Zealand is an unforgettable event in one of the world's most beautiful places.

▼ The rugged landscape of the North Island of New Zealand is on full display around Lake Taupo at the Kellog's Nutri-Grain IRONMAN New Zealand.

IRONMAN AUSTRALIA

Port Macquarie, Australia

QS: 40 for the same-year IRONMAN World Championship

Australia's oldest IRONMAN event, this race takes place in Port Maquarie in New South Wales, Australia. This superb course offers a unique challenge set along Port Macquarie's spectacular waterfront and throughout the scenic coastal region. Athletes swim the calm protected waters of Hastings river, ride along the Pacific Ocean, and run in the heart of Port Macquarie – a course renowned for its energetic sideline support from the local community.

▲ Port Macquarie's beautiful coastline provides the backdrop for the majority of the course.

IRONMAN ITALY, EMILIA-ROMAGNA
Cervia, Italy
QS: 40 for the next-year IRONMAN World Championship

On the coast of Emilia-Romagna – one of the most famous Italian regions in the world for nature, art, and food, just 15 miles from Ravenna – sits Cervia. This ancient fishing village, nicknamed the City of Salt, became known during the Roman Empire for its fine sand and wide centuries-old pinewood. In the 1800s, Cervia became an important tourist destination, and in 1912, the garden city of Milano Marittima was created, quickly becoming one of the most glamorous seaside towns in Italy. The IRONMAN adventure begins in the calm waters of Romagna, where athletes will take on the first 2.4 miles of the swim course. They will pass through the Natural Park of Salt Pens of Cervia, the habitat of pink flamingos, and cycle surrounded by history and nature. Finally, the marathon will take them through Cervia and Milano Marittima's most prominent landmarks, leading all athletes to the finish line.

▲ Athletes can feel as if they are stepping back in time as they race through the historic Italian countryside.

KMD IRONMAN COPENHAGEN
Copenhagen, Denmark
QS: 40 for the same-year IRONMAN World Championship

Copenhagen is one of the most colorful and energetic hosts on the European IRONMAN circuit, and this late-summer race never fails to disappoint athletes who flock there from all over the world. The course passes many of the picturesque city's historic landmarks, such as the world-famous Opera House, the Little Mermaid statue, Amalienborg Palace (home of the Danish Queen) and the New Harbour waterfront. The swim features a one-lap course in the lagoon at Amager Beach Park with excellent spectator views from the shores, as well as atop the three picturesque bridges perched above the action.

On the bike course, competitors will wind through central Copenhagen before heading north on two loops in the rolling hills of the island's northern countryside, where lush farmlands create a scenic tour. Athletes will find themselves in a Tour de France-like atmosphere with spectators lining the course. Once back in downtown Copenhagen, athletes will dismount their bikes next to the Royal Actress House. This might be the fastest T2 in the world, as athletes hand over their bike and begin the run in just over 50 seconds. The 4.5-loop run course takes in the city's harbor, lined with bright 17th and 18th-century row houses and more than 150,000 cheering fans.

▲ The relatively flat bike course is a perfect place to come for those athletes looking to set a PB on the bike leg.

2018 IRONMAN EVENTS

IRONMAN Arizona
IRONMAN Australia
IRONMAN Austria
IRONMAN Barcelona
IRONMAN Boulder
IRONMAN Brazil
IRONMAN Cairns
IRONMAN Canada
IRONMAN Chattanooga
IRONMAN Copenhagen
IRONMAN Cozumel
IRONMAN Florida
IRONMAN France

IRONMAN Frankfurt
IRONMAN Gurye
IRONMAN Hamburg
IRONMAN Italy/Emilia Romagna
IRONMAN Kalmar
IRONMAN Lake Placid
IRONMAN Lanzarote
IRONMAN Louisville
IRONMAN Maastricht
IRONMAN Maryland
IRONMAN Mont-Tremblant
IRONMAN New Zealand
IRONMAN Norway

IRONMAN Philippines
IRONMAN Santa Rosa
IRONMAN South Africa
IRONMAN Switzerland
IRONMAN Taiwan
IRONMAN Tallinn
IRONMAN Texas
IRONMAN UK
IRONMAN Vichy
IRONMAN Wales
IRONMAN Western Australia
IRONMAN Wisconsin

2018 IRONMAN 70.3 EVENTS

IRONMAN 70.3 Arizona
IRONMAN 70.3 Astana
IRONMAN 70.3 Atlantic City
IRONMAN 70.3 Augusta
IRONMAN 70.3 Barcelona
IRONMAN 70.3 Bariloche
IRONMAN 70.3 Bintan
IRONMAN 70.3 Boulder
IRONMAN 70.3 Buenos Aires
IRONMAN 70.3 Buffalo Springs Lake
IRONMAN 70.3 Busselton
IRONMAN 70.3 Cairns
IRONMAN 70.3 Calgary
IRONMAN 70.3 Campeche
IRONMAN 70.3 Canada
IRONMAN 70.3 Cebu
IRONMAN 70.3 Chattanooga
IRONMAN 70.3 Chongqing
IRONMAN 70.3 Coeur d'Alene
IRONMAN 70.3 Colombo
IRONMAN 70.3 Costa Rica
IRONMAN 70.3 Cozumel
IRONMAN 70.3 Davao
IRONMAN 70.3 Dubai
IRONMAN 70.3 Dun Laoghaire
IRONMAN 70.3 Durban
IRONMAN 70.3 Eagleman
IRONMAN 70.3 Ecuador
IRONMAN 70.3 Edinburgh
IRONMAN 70.3 Elsinore
IRONMAN 70.3 Finland
IRONMAN 70.3 Florianopolis

IRONMAN 70.3 Florida
IRONMAN 70.3 Gdynia
IRONMAN 70.3 Geelong
IRONMAN 70.3 Gulf Coast
IRONMAN 70.3 Hawaii
IRONMAN 70.3 Japan
IRONMAN 70.3 Jeju
IRONMAN 70.3 Jönköping
IRONMAN 70.3 Kraichgau
IRONMAN 70.3 Lake Placid
IRONMAN 70.3 Liuzhou
IRONMAN 70.3 Los Cabos
IRONMAN 70.3 Luxembourg
IRONMAN 70.3 Maceio
IRONMAN 70.3 Maine
IRONMAN 70.3 Mallorca
IRONMAN 70.3 Marbella
IRONMAN 70.3 Mont Tremblant
IRONMAN 70.3 Monterrey
IRONMAN 70.3 Muncie
IRONMAN 70.3 Muskoka
IRONMAN 70.3 New Zealand
IRONMAN 70.3 Nice
IRONMAN 70.3 Oceanside
IRONMAN 70.3 Ohio
IRONMAN 70.3 Otepää
IRONMAN 70.3 Pays d'Aix
IRONMAN 70.3 Peru
IRONMAN 70.3 Pescara
IRONMAN 70.3 Port Macquarie
IRONMAN 70.3 Portugal
IRONMAN 70.3 Pucon

IRONMAN 70.3 Puerto Rico
IRONMAN 70.3 Punta del Este
IRONMAN 70.3 Qujing
IRONMAN 70.3 Raleigh
IRONMAN 70.3 Rapperswil
IRONMAN 70.3 Rio de Janeiro
IRONMAN 70.3 Ruegen
IRONMAN 70.3 Santa Cruz
IRONMAN 70.3 Santa Rosa
IRONMAN 70.3 Slovenia
IRONMAN 70.3 South Africa
IRONMAN 70.3 St. George
IRONMAN 70.3 St. Polten
IRONMAN 70.3 Staffordshire
IRONMAN 70.3 Steelhead
IRONMAN 70.3 Sunshine Coast
IRONMAN 70.3 Superfrog
IRONMAN 70.3 Syracuse
IRONMAN 70.3 Taiwan
IRONMAN 70.3 Taupo
IRONMAN 70.3 Texas
IRONMAN 70.3 Vichy
IRONMAN 70.3 Victoria
IRONMAN 70.3 Vietnam
IRONMAN 70.3 Waco
IRONMAN 70.3 Western Australia
IRONMAN 70.3 Weymouth
IRONMAN 70.3 Wisconsin
IRONMAN 70.3 Xiamen
IRONMAN 70.3 Zell am See

IRONMAN 70.3 OCEANSIDE
Oceanside, California, USA
QS: 30 for the same-year IRONMAN 70.3 World Championship

Oceanside, California, offers triathletes a chance to race in the region that birthed the sport in the early 1970s in Mission Bay. Oceanside is located at the northern end of San Diego's North County, which includes the beach communities of Del Mar, Cardiff, Encinitas, and Carlsbad – home to surf, triathlon, and beach culture. Just half an hour south lies San Diego, with its world-famous zoo, parks, and other attractions to fill a spring break vacation. Just two hours away from the local mountains, skiing and snowboarding are other options.

This race offers one of the few chances athletes have to swim in the Oceanside Harbor, where water temperatures in early spring are usually in the low to mid 60s. The bike course takes cyclists along the California coastline to San Clemente, before dropping down into the Marine Corps Base Camp Pendleton. Here, challenging hills confront athletes before they swing back to the Oceanside Harbor. The run portion takes athletes on a winding journey out to Oceanside's flat beachfront path known as "The Strand," where miles of sandy beaches provide a beautiful and distracting vista. Runners then turn into a residential area before looping back out for a grand finish at the ocean's edge and a chute lined with energetic spectators.

▲Former IRONMAN champion Jan Frodeno runs past watching surfers on The Strand in 2018

▼Athletes dive into the lake during the rolling start at the 2015 IRONMAN 70.3 Coeur d'Alene.

IRONMAN 70.3 COEUR D'ALENE
Coeur d'Alene, Idaho, USA
QS: 30 for the same-year IRONMAN 70.3 World Championship

Another favorite on the IRONMAN 70.3 race circuit, this early-summer event takes place in the pristine heart of one of Idaho's prettiest areas – when the lush surrounding forest is starting to become very green. Coeur d'Alene is a classic resort and vacation destination that offers numerous recreational activities. The glacier-fed lake, surrounding forests and parks, the Trail of the Coeur d'Alenes and the Coeur d'Alene Resort Golf Course's floating green are just a few examples. Athletes begin their day with a 1.2-mile swim in the clear waters of Lake Coeur d'Alene. The challenging 56-mile bike course has many twists and turns. The run loops along the shores of the lake blending the energy of a small-town resort atmosphere with a world-class course.

IRONMAN 70.3 XIAMEN
Xiamen, China
QS: 25 for the next-year IRONMAN World Championship and 50 for the next-year IRONMAN 70.3 World Championship

Xiamen, the "Garden of the Sea," is a modern port city and a prestigious tourist destination located on the southeast coast of China. Here, sea views are backed by impressive cityscapes, offering a unique blend of the natural and urban. This coastal city is simultaneously ancient and modern, traditional and progressive, relaxation and revitalizing. The city of over 3 million has been named one of the most livable cities in China, and boasts an open economy and a diverse cultural profile. Since China's reform, Xiamen has sustained over three decades' worth of growth, and is expected to develop into a model city for the China of the future.

Adjacent to the convention and exhibition center are two five-star hotels: the Xiamen International Conference Center Hotel and Xiamen International Seaside Hotel. There is a vast array of other highly rated hotels in the area, offering abundant accommodation choices for the athletes and their spectators. The routes for the swim, bike, and run are all located just a short walk from the International Conference Center Hotel, and the area is easily accessible by all forms of transportation.

▼ The beautiful city of Xiamen, which combines the natural and urban world so effectively, plays host to the IRONMAN 70.3 Xiamen.

TRI-CLUBS CHAMPIONSHIPS

All registered IRONMAN TriClubs can compete in their TriClub Regional Championship. Championship scoring will be based on the Age Group Ranking system, however only the top five individual athlete results from each of the qualified clubs will be added together to receive a club grand total. The Club with the most points in each division will be crowned Regional TriClub Champion. In the event of a tie, the sixth ranked athlete for each club will be added to the total. Athletes will continue to be added until the tie is broken. Tri Club championships occur through the Regional Asian Regional TriClub Championship, the North American Regional Champoionship the EMEA Regional TRiClub Championship and the Latin America Regional TriClub Championship.

SPARKASSE IRONMAN 70.3 KRAICHGAU
Kraichgau, Germany
QS: 50 for the same-year IRONMAN 70.3 World Championship

The Kraichgau region in southwest Germany is a popular triathlon hotspot. Known as the land of the 1000 hills, the region offers everything: beautiful scenery, a demanding race course, and a culture representative of the sport. Thousands of spectators along the course make the race the ideal experience for every athlete. The swim takes place in the leisure area of Hardtsee, and the dynamic bike course offers fast sections and short climbs. One highlight is the big climb on the Schindelberg, where athletes will be treated to fantastic views of the Kraichgau region. The three-loop run course is a special experience, where thousands of spectators cheer enthusiastically.

▲ The bike course is incredibly varied, with both sprints through historic towns and climbs up challenging hills.

IRONMAN 70.3 PORTUGAL
Cascais, Portugal
QS: 50 for the next-year IRONMAN 70.3 World Championship

With its mild climate and 3,000 hours of sunshine per year, Portugal has always been the perfect destination for a holiday. The historic town of Cascais is just a short drive from Lisbon International Airport and is located between Sintra – a UNESCO World Heritage Site –and the village of Oeiras. On race day, athletes will experience the best Cascais has to offer, starting with a one loop swim in front of the Fortaleza da Cidadela, the most spectacular bay in Portugal. With its starting point in Cascais, the single-loop bike course runs alongside the ocean, through to Oeiras, Algés, and Belém, and returning in Alcântara, a fast and flat part of this beautiful landscape. The course also covers stunning natural scenery in the Sintra forests, returning to Cascais along the Guincho Beach road "where the land ends and the sea begins." The two loops of the run course start in the Hippodrome, taking athletes through Cascais Village. Historic houses, palaces, and fortresses of bygone times watch over one of the most beautiful race courses ever designed for a triathlon – this race is guaranteed to be among the most amazing experiences of an athlete's lifetime.

▲ The athletes dive into the warm coastal waters just after dawn at the start of the race.

THE BAKER INSTITUTE IRONMAN 70.3 GEELONG

Geelong, Victoria, Australia

QS: 30 for the same-year IRONMAN 70.3 World Championship

Victoria's oldest IRONMAN 70.3 takes place along Geelong's spectacular waterfront and throughout the scenic countryside. Athletes swim in the clear waters of Corio Bay, pit themselves against the fast, challenging bike course, and finish with a picturesque run along the waterfront. This waterfront city provides everything athletes need for the perfect race, possessing both the sophistication of a capital city and warmth of regional hospitality. Less than an hour's drive from Melbourne and Tullamarine Airport along the Princess Freeway, Geelong is beautifully placed with waterfront views of Corio Bay, immediate access to the world famous Great Ocean Road, and the charming wine growing region of the Bellarine. The city's multi-million-dollar Waterfront Geelong features many cafés and restaurants, fully restored art deco seawater baths, a yacht club marina, and a scenic bay side promenade.

▲ Swim, bike and run: the course in Geelong provides a challenge for every IRONMAN athlete.

KÖLBI IRONMAN 70.3 COSTA RICA

Playa del Coco, Costa Rica

QS: 30 for the same-year IRONMAN 70.3 World Championship

Costa Rica is one of the world's most unique tourist destinations. The natural beauty, stunning beaches, pleasant climate and the peaceful easy going nature of Costa Ricans make the country an attractive, must see part of the world. In Costa Rica, athletes get to experience tropical ecosystems, vast vegetation, pleasant climate, topography, insects and birds. The country protects approximately 26 percent of its national territory in national parks, wildlife reserves, forest preserves and private reserves. This race is best-loved by athletes for its swim in the crystal clear waters of the Pacific between corral reef and fish of thousand colors. Spectators can watch the entire swim from the beautiful Playa del Coco, with its incredible bay surrounded by sailboats and fishing boats. On the bike, athletes take in the foliage cover of the jungle on a fast yet challenging course frequented by monkeys and iguanas. The run takes place along the "Paseo del Amor" (Love Walk), and is one of the enthusiastic routes on the South American circuit.

▲ Excited athletes prepare themselves at the start of the race before entering the warm waters of the Pacific Ocean.

SHORT COURSE TRI

When thinking of IRONMAN, the first image most see is the full-blown, sinew-straining effort of the IRONMAN World Championship course in Kailua-Kona, Hawaii, or one of many IRONMAN 70.3 events. But there are shorter races to be conquered, too.

For example, there is the International Triathlon Union (ITU) World Triathlon in Abu Dhabi, staged in partnership with IRONMAN. This includes a variety of courses depending on age and ability, among them a half-mile swim, 2.5-mile cycle ride and 1.5-mile run. The distances are manageable, but temperatures can reach highs of 84°F, which present their own challenges to participants more familiar with cooler climates.

Another option is to return to the place where triathlon began back in the early 1970s: Coronado, near San Diego. This is where John and Judy Collins first experienced the sport that they would soon revolutionize, and it is here that the U.S. Special Forces – the legendary NAVY SEALs – go to compete. Anyone can attempt to beat them as the events held here are open to seasoned athletes and first-timers alike. The SUPERSEAL Olympic triathlon and the SEAL Sprint triathlon are held on the same day, using essentially the same course.

The Olympic event centers on Silver Strand State Beach, with a mile swim in the bay's calm waters which average around 57°F. The 25-mile cycle route is flat and fast on Highway 75 and there is a one-loop out-and-back 6-mile dirt trail run to round things off. The sprint edition is roughly half the distance, with a half-mile swim, 12.5-mile bike and 3.75-mile run.

▼ No matter what length a triathlon is, all of the athletes give everything they have.

IRONKIDS

▲ IRONKIDS Wales hosts 1,000 children for a race in Tenby, Wales. It is just one of the many events IRONMAN holds for children each year.

Taking part in an IRONMAN event is about learning how to overcome something that may not have originally seemed possible. This is a lesson that can take many people a whole lifetime to understand, but the IRONKIDS races strive to help children along this path as early as possible. The main purpose of these events is to help kids develop a sense of good health, an appreciation of the fun aspects of exercise and – maybe – breed the next generation of IRONMAN World Champions in the process.

Like its parent events, IRONKIDS has grown from small beginnings into a global series of well-attended events. There are now more than 80 races from Argentina to Vietnam, taking place in Europe, the Middle East, the Americas and going all around the world to New Zealand and Australia.

The emphasis for the younger participants is on taking part, having fun and being active and positive. Healthy kids have a better chance of being healthy adults, and it is worth bearing in mind that risk factors for chronic illnesses such as heart disease, high blood pressure and type-2 diabetes can all take root in the adolescent years. Children who undertake regular physical activity have better cardiovascular fitness, stronger bones and muscles, lower body fat and can have fewer symptoms of anxiety and depression.

At every age, the frequency, intensity, length and mix of activities are important. Weight-bearing exercises like running and jumping are always crucial though, helping to build healthy bones, especially in the teen years when the greatest gains in bone mass occur.

IRONKIDS focuses on getting a feel for different events while enjoying the experience.

It's easy to find a race anywhere in the world, and they often take place at the same time as the IRONMAN and IRONMAN 70.3 events. This makes them ideal companion pieces for parents who are entering the adult version – the whole family can take part together, allowing everyone to come away from the weekend having been part of the IRONMAN experience. Finishers can look forward to receiving goodies that include items such as medals or t-shirts and prizes for those who place at the top.

IRONKIDS races are always age appropriate; they provide a healthy and achievable challenge. When the kids are very young, it may be possible for the adults to accompany them, but it's not always allowed for the older groups. By the age of nine, children start to develop the coordination needed to participate in organized sports.

In addition to hosting a race just for kids, each location may feature additional attractions such as an expo where the children can try out products, learn more about nutrition and how to progress in triathlon. IRONMAN has also offered clinics in the run-up to races to give a basic idea of training for newcomers. Some races have also featured mini film festivals.

Dip 'n' Dash, an event for youngsters that combines a swim with a run, has become more popular in recent years. Some IRONKIDS and IRONMAN events include a Dip 'n' Dash alongside the main event. But whether it's a run on its own, a triathlon or a swim and a run, the friendly atmosphere and excitement of race day will, with any luck, shape a whole life of healthy and active living. There's no excuse for anyone in the family to miss out on taking part in an IRONMAN weekend.

▲ The 2016 IRONKIDS Xiamen event included a warm-up session with the legendary IRONMAN champion Craig Alexander to inspire the budding athletes.

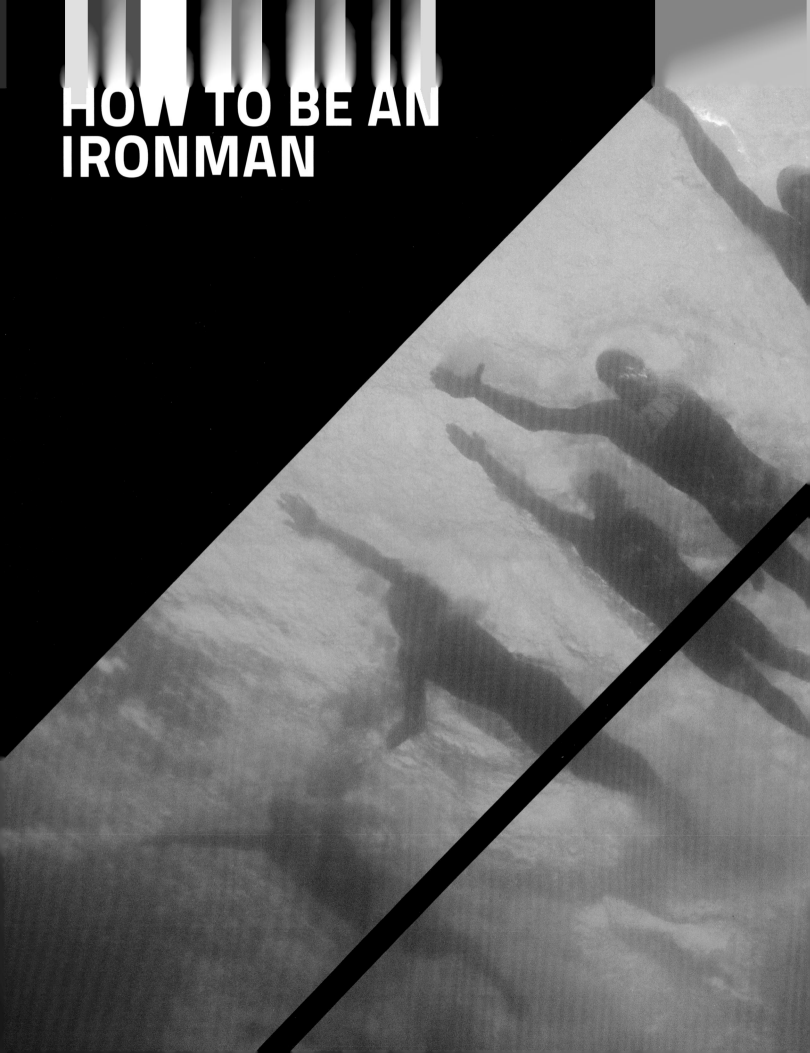

HOW TO BE AN IRONMAN

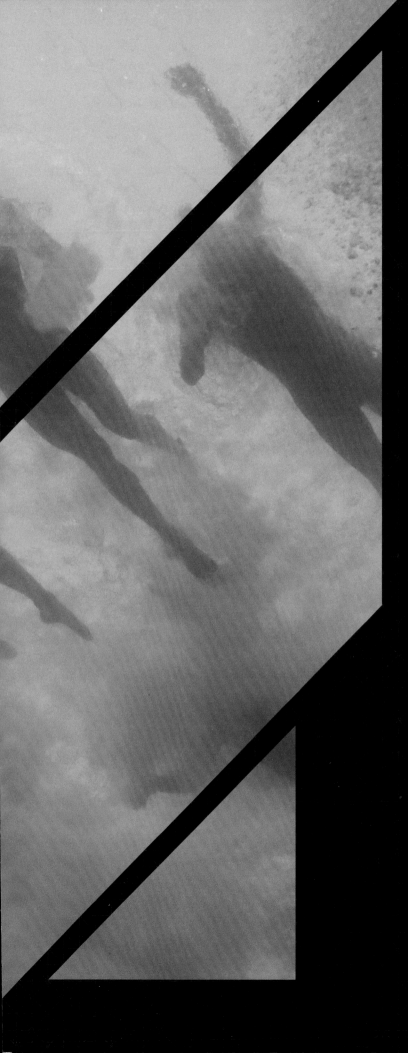

The IRONMAN ethos is all about helping athletes on the journey towards crossing both the start and finish lines for the first time, even those who thought they would never be able to do it. Whether old or young, a first-timer or a veteran, able-bodied or physically challenged, there is no bar to who can participate in IRONMAN® events.

◀An underwater photograph of swimmers competing at the 2017 IRONMAN World Championship

IRONMAN can motivate all types of athletes, from those who are preparing for their first triathlon, to those who have their hearts set on qualifying for the IRONMAN World Championship. "IRONMAN Around the World" has shown there is no shortage of spectacular events to choose from. The ironman.com website is a great resource for information about all the races that IRONMAN has to offer.

The key to tackling an IRONMAN® race is to remember that perspective is of the utmost importance. What might first seem unimaginable can, with focus, positive thinking, and the ability to break down the challenge into smaller components, become manageable. One aspect of the preparation experience is guaranteed – every IRONMAN athlete must complete sufficient training.

The level and quantity needed is difficult to predict – it varies for each athlete and there's no real "average" training plan for an IRONMAN event (in fact, there's nothing "average" about an IRONMAN athlete, no matter the level). But it is recommended that triathletes begin to prepare seven months before an IRONMAN event. The number of hours an amateur athlete can train for an

▼ Athletes charge out of the sea and towards the transition area during a triathlon in 2017 in Bergen, Germany.

IRONMAN 70.3 is 8 hours per week, and an IRONMAN is 12 hours per week.

Because of the format of the race itself, it is important that an athlete trains adequately in each of the three disciplines: swim, bike, and run. Those who are concerned about a lack of experience can ease their fears with the knowledge that 40 percent of the field at an IRONMAN event consists of first-timers. With the appropriate level of training, attention to nutrition, and mental preparedness, there is no reason why anybody should lack confidence when approaching the start line come race day.

"If you set a goal for yourself and are able to achieve it, you have won your race. Your goal can be to come in first, to improve your performance, or just to finish; it's up to you."

DAVE SCOTT, SIX-TIME IRONMAN WORLD CHAMPION AND HALL OF FAME INDUCTEE

Who is an IRONMAN?

% Male / % Female:	68 / 32
Average Athlete Age:	40 years
University Educated:	92%

The race that everyone is most familiar with is, of course, the IRONMAN World Championship held in Kailua-Kona, Hawai`i. Even the most single-minded athletes need a mixture of skill, luck and dogged determination to make it happen. Each year, more than 80,000 athletes vie for "slots" at qualifying IRONMAN events worldwide, but only around 2,400 make it to the starting line. However, qualifying is only one of the available options for aspiring athletes to make their route to Kona.

BEGINNER'S GEAR

▲ Part of the goal of swim training is to prepare athletes for finishing the swim leg with plenty of energy for the rest of the race.

SWIM

There are only a few essentials for beginning swim training for a triathlon. Every athlete should own at least two swimsuits designed for sport. Next, there are several different styles and makes of goggles. Participants should test a few pairs in race conditions while in training to ensure their goggles fit and function properly on race day. Other necessary equipment includes swim caps, a water bottle, a padlock for the locker, and a towel.

As race day approaches, it is recommended to have at least two pairs of goggles, swimsuits and swim caps for pre-race practice sessions, a wetsuit (or swimskin for non-wetsuit legal races, which is placed over the triathlon suit and removed after the swim), and a watch.

BIKE

There are many factors to consider when choosing the right bike, but many coaches and athletes alike will agree that the most important is comfort. Most local bike shops will take an athlete's measurements and test their flexibility in order to recommend bike options best suited to their physical frame and riding style. Many shops also allow bikes to be tested out on the road. The aesthetic of a bike should not be a major factor in the final decision; IRONMAN athletes should buy the bike that best fits their individual needs. After all, it will be their partner on the road for thousands of miles.

Swim Training Basics

- Kick board (many pools will have these available)
- Pull buoy (this will assist with pull sets, also available at many pool facilities)
- Paddles (available in varying sizes – the larger they are, the harder the workout)
- Swim bag (helpful for carrying gear from the locker to the water)
- Bathing suit
- Goggles
- Stopwatch

Some athletes may choose to purchase a triathlon-specific bike, but if the bike will be used for other types of cycling then a normal road bike might be the best option. Road bikes allow the cyclist to sit more upright and further back on the saddle. These bikes are also versatile: clip-on aero bars can be added, for example, among other adjustments. Aero bars are narrow, bolt-on extensions that help to draw the cyclist's body forward into a more aerodynamic position. On the other hand, the advantage of a triathlon-specific bike is built-in aerodynamics and other race-specific features.

As IRONMAN Certified Coach, Carrie Barrett writes:

"Aluminum and steel frames [...] are durable, sturdy and less expensive than carbon frames. They are a great option for the budget-conscious beginner cyclist. Carbon fiber components and frames are lighter and tend to absorb more road vibration, making for a smoother ride."

The type of bike will ultimately be influenced by how serious the athlete is about improving his or her time. Barrett wrote of her early years, "Like most, I knew I wanted to complete sprint triathlons and some weekend recreational riding, but I didn't have grand visions of riding the Tour de France. I wasn't concerned about speed as much as I was about having fun and being safe [...] after several years, I knew I was hooked and ready to upgrade to a full carbon tri bike."

Cycling knowledge along with experience will also help determine the type of bike to purchase. There are other important questions to consider when choosing the right bike, such as: one's comfort level riding in a pack; whether clip-in pedals, which require specialized shoes, are an option; the ease of making on-the-road repairs, for example, changing a flat tire; and to what extent a multitude of gear change options are an integral part of the racing plan. Ultimately, competence builds confidence. The bike that feels the safest is often the right choice.

◀ A serious competitor should pay attention to everything from aero bars and clip-in pedals to clothing and the helmet.

RUN

Running shoes are the most important piece of gear for the run. A visit to a running specific store can be very useful, especially when it comes to receiving advice on which shoes best suit an athlete who will be running for such long distances. The better outlets offer analysis of running styles on a machine hooked up to a computer, which further helps to pinpoint the correct footwear. A good pair of socks is also of utmost importance over long distances. Other kit items include shorts and running t-shirts or singlets (and warmer gear if training through winter), a sports bra (for women), sunglasses, a hat or visor, and sunscreen (depending on the location and time of year). Energy gels are a necessary part of the modern racing experience. With a selection of energy gels available, it is suggested that athletes experiment with different gels in training to discover which offer the best boost.

Other non-essential items include a hand-held water bottle or a water belt, which can be helpful on long runs, particularly when running through rural areas or other routes that don't take the runner past sources of water. A GPS watch can also be a great tool for tracking performance levels, and when paired with a heart-rate monitor, these devices provide all the statistics imaginable. Anti-chafing cream and an MP3 player (not allowed on race day) can be useful for training as well. It is important to test all equipment while in training to avoid any unexpected challenges on race day.

TRAINING

Once the equipment is purchased, it is time to start the training. Here are some words of wisdom from IRONMAN World Champion and Hall of Famer Lori Bowden on each of the three disciplines. First, the swim:

Race-Day Run Checklist

- Race bib belt
- Hat or visor
- Sunglasses
- Sunscreen
- Watch
- Race nutrition products (gels, sports drinks and salt tabs, as per training and personal needs)
- Post-race clothing

"The people still left at this point, they're possessed of just one thing – finishing. They're saying to themselves: 'If I can be standing at the finish I've won.' And they're right."

ACTOR BRUCE DERN ON THE LAST FEW MILES OF THE IRONMAN WORLD CHAMPIONSHIP, SPEAKING ON THE ROAD WHILE RUNNING THE QUEEN K HIGHWAY IN 1982

"After training with Neil Harvey, an amazing swim coach, I had great improvements. Even when my swim times weren't super fast, I came out of the water less tired, and also learned to love swimming. Swimming wasn't my best, but I learned to try and swim as well as possible each race. Funny, now swimming is one of the things I miss the most [about competition]."

Second, the bike:

"I loved long bike rides – the longer, the better. If I went for a seven-hour ride it made the IRONMAN bike leg feel so much shorter. In races, the hillier the course the better; I'd much rather go up a hill than down.

And, third, the run:

"The run, I loved. When I started the run in each race I was so incredibly happy to just be running. If my legs weren't great when I started the run, I knew they must start feeling better at some point. I knew on a good day I could run very fast and on a bad day, if I just kept moving, I could still have a good run."

◀ Lionel Sanders showcases useful gear for the marathon run.

THINK FOOD

Nutrition is a vital aspect of both training and racing. What athletes put inside their bodies – their fuel – is just as important as the extreme training hours accumulated. Good nutritional practice should not only be a priority on a heavy training day, but every day. As IRONMAN U Master Coach Matt Dixon has said, many of the incremental gains in the sport are built on successful basic habits. A key component to progressing in triathlon is ensuring that athletes' most basic habits are part of their everyday regime. Dixon shared some great advice around general eating, as opposed to the calories consumed in and around exercise:

"This is an area that I personally believe is made entirely too complicated with so many experts (and faux-experts) promoting all sorts of miracle cures and diets that claim to trim fat, boost energy, and provide some magic elixir for a better life. As a general rule of thumb – don't believe the bunk! And don't make it overly complicated."

Eat plenty: the overwhelming majority of training hours demand a solid number of daily calories as support as well as to allow for recovery and adaptations. "You need to be an eating machine," writes Dixon.

Avoid sugar: the massive increase in sugar intake over the last generation has been a health disaster all over the developed world. Avoid packaged and processed foods and restrict sugary drinks and sweets.

Eat protein and fats: the foundation of a quality diet includes a quality protein source and fat with every single meal. This means plenty of healthy oils – avoid vegetable and other processed oils – avocados, nuts, and seeds in support of meat, fish and other lean proteins.

Eat nutritious carbohydrates: avoid too much bread, pasta and starchy carbohydrates and instead focus on carbohydrates that hold high nutrient value. This includes quinoa, amaranth, vegetables and fruits.

Moderation: don't be a slave to your plan. Occasionally, enjoy treats such as pizza, pasta, and wine, but don't make it a regular occurrence.

Breakfast: Dixon writes, "I believe breakfast is the foundation of successful daily eating. Make it a habit to always eat a healthy breakfast and make it your largest meal of the day. My favorite breakfast tip: if you like oatmeal, which is a great choice, add blackstrap molasses to it as your sweetener. It's a great source of iron,

calcium and magnesium and, while it is an acquired taste, if it was good enough for my ancestors (well, my dad), then it must be great for me… surely."

Conceptually, this all appears very simple, but there are plans available to give additional structure, if needed. However, beware: "Avoid falling for any of the promotions in books," advises Dixon, "but draw from them for structure and recipe ideas." Of course, it goes without saying, that the best way to remove any doubt about a plan is to seek professional guidance from a coach or a sports nutritionist.

TRAINING TIME REQUIREMENTS

▲ Age should not be a barrier to compete in IRONMAN events, as 80-year-old New Zealander Garth Barfoot proved upon finishing an IRONMAN 70.3 in 2016.

Long-course racing is the fastest-growing segment in the sport of triathlon, and the IRONMAN and IRONMAN 70.3 series offer the widest range of options for aspiring triathletes.

Competitors considering racing the 140.6-mile IRONMAN triathlon face a very unique challenge, which requires time and commitment. However, those willing to commit to the training time to be successful usually are. The cut-off time for the event is 17 hours for most events, including the IRONMAN World Championship; athletes must cross the finish line before this in order to have officially finished the race. The elite athletes approach the 8- to 9-hour mark, while top age-groupers normally cover the ground in less than 10 hours, depending on the race.

Of course, the dream of competing in the lava fields of Kailua-Kona has become a major motivation in the sport for athletes around the world, leading many to pursue the longer, bigger time-commitment race of the IRONMAN events. However, some still prefer the short distance on offer in IRONMAN 70.3.

IRONMAN 70.3 races still provide challenges for athletes, but with a lower overall time commitment. In many ways, IRONMAN 70.3 events are just as competitive as IRONMAN races. IRONMAN 70.3 includes a larger population of athletes because of the time management and training regiment compared to an IRONMAN. Athletes all around the world travel to IRONMAN and IRONMAN 70.3 race weekends to compete in these events.

No matter your goals, there are time commitments required to complete either an IRONMAN 70.3 or IRONMAN triathlon.

When first considering competing, talk with an experienced athlete, not only about their training methodologies, but how they balance training with their daily responsibilities, such as work and family. You'll find many creative answers, and quickly learn that triathlon is a positive addition to even the busiest schedules. Whether looking to be competitive or simply finish, the amount of training required will be related to the goals, age, and athletic background of the athlete. The loftier their ambitions, the more they will need to prioritize their training. The closer they are to a podium place, the smaller the margins of error become, and small gains can mean big breakthroughs.

The older an athlete, the more aging affects their ability to recover from strenuous training. There is a point at which breakdown occurs from training for all athletes, and Father Time is a big factor in the amount of training required and recommended for older athletes.

ATHLETIC BACKGROUND

An athlete's background determines a degree of the success they can expect when first getting into triathlon. Someone who has been an avid swimmer, cyclist, or runner most of their life will have a good starting fitness base. Each different background has its advantages and disadvantages, when it comes to being immediately successful in an IRONMAN triathlon. Table 1 outlines the general advantages each sporting background provides.

For those who have never been active, and are in effect attempting serious training for the first time, the challenges will be greater. However, there isn't any reason to believe that over time both success and enjoyment can't be achieved. With consistent training and racing, big improvements in performance and training are absolutely certain to come.

There are also IRONMAN athletes who begin training having come from a background of playing an entirely different sport, such as soccer, baseball, golf, lacrosse, or many others. While it is hard to quantify each one of these sports, in general, the more athleticism the athlete has developed in their time before entering

triathlon, the more likely they will pick up the sport quickly and see big gains in fitness, skill and performance. Even an older athlete, who perhaps cannot train as much as a younger athlete, may still be able to perform better based on their background coming into the sport, and how long they have been previously active.

Table 1

ATHLETE BACKGROUND	ADVANTAGES
Swimmer	• Swim skill already likely high • Low training volume needed to keep skill and fitness, can focus on other two disciplines
Cyclist	• Past training volume likely already high • Bike is approximately 50% of the race time, most of the three sports
Runner	• Strong fitness base, reduced running volume needed • Injury risks reduced • Run is approximately 25–35% of the race time

◀ Female athletes power themselves uphill at the 2017 IRONMNAN 70.3 World Championship in Chattanooga, Tennessee.

SETTING GOALS

Once an athlete has considered their background and where their strengths and weaknesses might lie, it is time to determine their goals, before meshing their goals and background together to form a training program. Athletes can be classified into three basic groups (in box below), based on goals. These groups are:

FINISHER

These athletes often simply enjoy the challenge of covering the distance, as well as the training and camaraderie that triathlon provides. Training to finish an IRONMAN or IRONMAN 70.3 is no small thing, and brings about many positive lifestyle changes for many new athletes. For this level of athlete, the finish line is a celebration of newly acquired fitness, and commitment to a training regimen. Some athletes in this category, however, still have dreams of achieving various personal goals.

COMPETITIVE AGE-GROUPER

These athletes aren't just satisfied with finishing, they want to get faster and continue to get closer to the podium or top ten percent of their age group. These athletes often display a high level of commitment to their training. They tend to do longer and more frequent training sessions, as well as ones that are harder and more intense.

WORLD CHAMPIONSHIP QUALIFIER

These athletes are the ones who are consistently racing at the front of their division or age-group, and are looking to win the race, finish on the podium, and/or qualify for the IRONMAN World Championship. These athletes are extremely dedicated to accomplishing their goals, and training and racing are a priority in their daily lives.

Tables 2 and 4 list the range of weekly training hours common among each goal-group per discipline, and the total hours per week. It should be noted that the ranges are quite wide because training times should vary depending on age and background. It is also common for an athlete to quickly move up or down a group, either because of the swift progress they make, or because of a change in lifestyle that may or may not allow training and racing to be prioritized.

Another way to view training is to see the frequency of training for each type of athlete, per discipline of the sport, (swim, bike or run), based on goals. Table 3 and 5 lists the range of training session frequency per week for each type of athlete for both.

Table 2 – IRONMAN 70.3 weekly training hours per discipline, based on athlete goals. The red fill indicates the suggested number of training hours per week, so a finisher should aim to complete between 1.5 and 3 hours of swim training each week.

ATHLETE GOALS	SWIM TRAINING HRS	BIKE TRAINING HRS	RUN TRAINING HRS	TOTAL HRS/WK
Finisher	1 2 3 4 5 6 7 8	2 4 6 8 10 12	1 2 3 4 5 6 7	4 8 12 16 20 28
Competitive Age-Grouper	1 2 3 4 5 6 7 8	2 4 6 8 10 12	1 2 3 4 5 6 7	4 8 12 16 20 28
World Championship Qualifier	1 2 3 4 5 6 7 8	2 4 6 8 10 12	1 2 3 4 5 6 7	4 8 12 16 20 28

Table 3 – IRONMAN 70.3 weekly training sessions per discipline, based on athlete goals. The red fill indicates the suggested number of training sessions per week, so a finisher should aim to complete between 1 and 3 sessions of swim training each week.

ATHLETE GOALS	SWIM TRAINING SESSIONS	BIKE TRAINING SESSIONS	RUN TRAINING SESSIONS	TOTAL SESSIONS/WK
Finisher	1 2 3 4 5 6	1 2 3 4 5 6	1 2 3 4 5 6 7	3 6 9 12 15 18
Competitive Age-Grouper	1 2 3 4 5 6	1 2 3 4 5 6	1 2 3 4 5 6 7	3 6 9 12 15 18
World Championship Qualifier	1 2 3 4 5 6	1 2 3 4 5 6	1 2 3 4 5 6 7	3 6 9 12 15 18

It might surprise many athletes to learn that though the distance doubles for racing, the training requirements and time commitment do not double. As training volume increases, the risk of injury increases as well, so it's important for athletes to stick to their plan and listen to their coaches and/or trainers. Athletes need to recognize they have to build slowly to the right volume for their goals and performance needs.

Table 4 – IRONMAN weekly training hours per discipline, based on athlete goals. The red fill indicates the suggested number of training hours per week, so a finisher should aim to complete between 2.5 and 4 hours of swim training each week.

ATHLETE GOALS	SWIM TRAINING HRS	BIKE TRAINING HRS	RUN TRAINING HRS	TOTAL HRS/WK
Finisher	2 4 6 8 10	3 6 9 12 15 18	2 4 6 8 10	6 12 18 24 30 36 42
Competitive Age-Grouper	2 4 6 8 10	3 6 9 12 15 18	2 4 6 8 10	6 12 18 24 30 36 42
World Championship Qualifier	2 4 6 8 10	3 6 9 12 15 18	2 4 6 8 10	6 12 18 24 30 36 42

Table 5 – IRONMAN weekly training sessions per discipline, based on athlete goals. The red fill indicates the suggested number of training sessions per week, so a finisher should aim to complete between 3 and 4 sessions of swim training each week.

ATHLETE GOALS	SWIM TRAINING SESSIONS	BIKE TRAINING SESSIONS	RUN TRAINING SESSIONS	TOTAL SESSIONS/WK
Finisher	1 2 3 4 5 6 7	1 2 3 4 5 6	1 2 3 4 5 6 7	4 8 12 16 20
Competitive Age-Grouper	1 2 3 4 5 6 7	1 2 3 4 5 6	1 2 3 4 5 6 7	4 8 12 16 20
World Championship Qualifier	1 2 3 4 5 6 7	1 2 3 4 5 6	1 2 3 4 5 6 7	4 8 12 16 20

Once an athlete knows their goals, and has a sense of their background, they can begin to plan training sessions and hours of training to address their weaknesses. These decisions should also take into consideration the course demands. For example, a hilly course is generally going to be more challenging than a flat course, meaning more time out on the course in the bike and run sections.

Though these tables simplify the approach to training for many, there are still supplemental training considerations to be made, outside of simple swim, bike and run training. These are not listed in Table 2 or 3, because they vary in time and frequency greatly to each athlete, again based on age, goals and background.

Strength training is vital for many athletes' long-term health, and to combat the effects of aging. The older the athlete and the higher their goals, the more important strength training becomes, and it needs to be inserted into a training plan.

Massage therapy and injury treatment can vary again based on the athlete, but also vary because of the time of year and how risky training is during a particular phase, creating a large training stress-load on the soft-tissues of the body. Massage therapy treatment can range from a few times per year, to a few per week. The older an athlete is, and the more on the brink of injury they might be, the more important this type of treatment becomes, although it is not effective for injuries to bones and ligaments. Injuries to bones and ligaments require a more serious approach to recovery and rehabilitation, generally under the guidance of doctors and licensed physical therapists.

▼ It is important to tailor training to the course that will be raced. For example, if it is a hilly course, ensure tricky ascents are included in bike training.

IMPORTANT TRAINING APPROACHES

Getting training right is probably the biggest challenge in the entire sport of triathlon. The athletes who get it right will find they have big advantages over their competition. They are the athletes that always peak at the right time of the year, when the races matter the most. They race well consistently, see steady improvement through the season, and also continue to improve season after season. They are rarely injured, and somehow never seem to suffer a setback, mentally or physically. The three best ways to become one of these athletes are to address the consistency of your training, your health and injury risk, and remember a key training rule: the 2-Day Rule.

CONSISTENCY OF TRAINING

There is no magic formula, or training plan, that can be devised and executed that makes up for a lack of consistent training for an athlete. Fitness gains are small in nature, while fitness losses are nearly exponential in comparison. Many top coaches and exercise physiologists believe athletes lose fitness at a rate which is nearly three times as fast as they gain it; forgo training for three days in a row and the fitness loss will already be noticeable. How much fitness is lost depends on the prior fitness level, but in general the fitter the athlete, the greater the loss.

On the other hand, obtaining long-term and large fitness gains requires a long-term and consistent commitment to training. The best athletes in the world have been training for the sport for many years – some even decades – consistently.

Below are some of the most common factors that negatively affect athlete consistency, and solutions to address them:

- **Frequent Sickness** – This is a sign that an athlete is over-reaching in training to the point that their immune system is compromised. Look for patterns in training, which may be leading to

sickness. If sickness usually follows a big-volume week, or travel for work, then there's a need to recognize those issues and plan better for them.

- **Injuries** – This is generally a sign that an athlete is increasing their load too quickly, or some type of trauma has occurred, perhaps not even training-related. Planning for the correct training dosages – and allowing for proper recovery – is of the utmost importance to maintain consistency and see fitness improvements. Be safe: traumatic injuries can cost months of training, while taking risks at high speed on the bike will provide little benefit.

- **Motivation** – Usually, this means the athlete has been so focused on training, and/or has subjected themselves to such a big training stress-load over a long duration, that they are no longer excited for training or racing. Plan two separate one-week breaks (at a minimum) per year. This allows not only the body to recuperate, but also the mind. This is usually best done after a peak event, or a big racing block of peak events.

- **Life Stress** – When an athlete is under large stress in their life, training tends to take a back seat. A lot of athletes use this as a reason to avoid training, instead of recognizing training can help them better handle the stress they are under, keeping the routine and their goals within reach.

- **Travel** – Traveling always makes training difficult, especially if regularly in unfamiliar areas. Nowadays, there are many resources available online that help athletes better plan for training while on the road. This includes hotels with full gym rooms, lap pools, local spin classes, running facilities, and also cycling routes and masters swim opportunities.

HEALTH AND INJURIES

The health of an athlete affects consistency and progress with training and fitness, and injuries or other setbacks are often avoidable and self-inflicted. Despite this, nearly every athlete will face an injury at some point, and the worst part lies in the knowledge that the injury could likely have been avoided.

The challenge of training is that it is predicated on the need to fatigue the body, in order to stimulate fitness gains and adaptations to those stimuli, but not to push it too much. Without fatigue, there is no improvement in fitness or stimulus. The imbalance of stimulus and response is the biggest error athletes and coaches tend to make. Most injuries can be avoided with a better, more balanced approach of stimulus and recovery.

This concept, although easy to think about in theory, is hard to put into practical application, especially for triathlon. This is because there are three different sports to monitor, and because each athlete's background and individuality must be taken into account. Even the same athlete's ability to recover changes with age and experience, or even with life-stress outside of sport and training. It is important to be responsive to the body's needs at all times.

THE 2-DAY RULE

One of the best ways to keep consistency of training, and to avoid many of the pitfalls discussed above, is to never dig the body into too deep of a hole. But how can an athlete or coach know if a hole is too deep to recover properly from?

A simple rule, called the 2-Day Rule, is a clear way to answer this question. If an athlete needs more than two days of recovery to return to a normal training level, then they have probably been digging too deep during training, and not allowing for enough recovery to have successful workouts. This likely means the training is risky enough to cause injury as well.

With two days of full recovery, light training and/or active recovery, an athlete should by the third day be extremely successful in outputs relative to their goals. The workouts on the day after the two light days should be some of the best of the year if set-up to be such an opportunity. If they aren't, then the approach to training needs to be re-examined for better balance of stress and recovery.

How often should these two light days be utilized? Making that decision is the art of coaching! The choice of when to rest is as important as what workouts to do. In general, whenever the athlete feels the load they are under is too big, and especially if workouts consistently aren't going as well as one would like, then it is the time to insert a two-day recovery block.

This rule addresses the mental and emotional aspect of training and racing as well. If an athlete hasn't seen success in training, how can they be expected to bring any confidence to their racing performances? They can't.

The 2-Day Rule allows the athlete to manage the physical stress and be sure they are confident and ready to race when on the start line.

▶ The training pays off: athletes compete at the 2017 IRONMAN 70.3 Liuzhou in China.

TRAINING YEAR AND PREPARATION

The duration of time from when an athlete begins their training and preparation to their final major peak event is called the "training year." For some athletes this lasts 8 to 10 months, while for others it can be even shorter.

The training year is divided into a few basic training periods, where the training focus changes. The beginning period is typically more basic in its fitness and skill building. This is often called the Base Period, or General Preparation. In this phase of training, athletes simply want to build the basic aerobic endurance and skills to be able to complete a more rigorous training protocol later on in the training year.

This phase can vary quite considerably in length. It first depends on the athlete's fitness level at the start of this phase, and second on how long until the peak event that they are aiming for. It is commonly believed that 14 weeks out from an event, an athlete needs to begin to make their training more reflective of the specific race demands. This is often referred to as the Specific Phase, or Build Phase, since athletes are building toward a specific race event. Anything before this 14-week period should still be considered part of the General Preparation phase. At that point, the athletes should focus on their weaknesses, and the things that will help them take the next step when the Specific Phase starts.

WHAT DOES GENERAL PREPARATION PHASE TRAINING LOOK LIKE?
It depends on the athlete and their goals. An athlete with an "IRONMAN finisher" goal might just be working on basic aerobic endurance, and never really have to change type of training much, but rather just keep adding aerobic volume.

For an elite athlete, the training would be similar, but perhaps contain more sprinting, high turnover work, strength in the weight room, and also more items that aren't directly related to race performance, but that still need to be addressed for an athlete to continue to develop and perform at the highest levels.

WHAT DOES SPECIFIC PREPARATION PHASE TRAINING LOOK LIKE?
Again, it depends on the goals of the athlete. An "IRONMAN finisher" might not see much difference between the General and Specific, just longer swims, rides and runs. Maybe if the race has a big climb, these athletes should include more climbing routes in their training rides. These athletes will also practice and train with their race-day nutrition, perfecting the nutrition strategy, and race in the conditions that will most likely be faced on race day, e.g. heat, humidity, or colder temperatures.

For an elite, this would include long rides paced at race intensity, likely with intervals, and based on the strategy they plan to execute during the race. This might even include some bike attacks on a climb, or swim workouts based on the mass start and fast sprints to get into the front pack.

When the 14-week period before your peak event begins, training should change to represent the demands specific to the race itself. These demands often come from the type of course being used or the race conditions. Can this phase start before 14 weeks? Yes, but that becomes very risky, so athletes need to pay attention that they haven't begun the specific training phase too soon, or the body's fitness will peak before the race, and not improve in the weeks leading into the race. Worse, the athlete could begin to regress. Athletes who try to do the same training approach year-round tend to see this happen quite often.

When athletes have a second peak event that is less than two months from the prior peak event, the plan should be initially to recover from the first race, before beginning again with a specific training phase, even if that leaves only a very brief time of a few weeks, or even days.

The biggest thing to remember is that training decisions are always made based on the goals of the athlete, and what it will require to achieve those goals.

DIFFERENT APPROACHES TO TRAINING INTENSITIES

▶ Figure 1: Borg 1998 perceived exertion scale. (Borg RPE scale © Gunnar Borg, 1970, 1985, 1994, 1998)

NUMBER	LEVEL OF EXERTION
6	No exertion at all
7	
7.5	Extremely light
8	
9	Very light
10	
11	Light
12	
13	Somewhat hard
14	
15	Hard
16	
17	Very hard
18	
19	Extremely hard
20	Maximal exertion

For the pioneer athletes, training for IRONMAN racing had to be mostly based on feel and heart-rate based efforts. These two approaches are still very common today but, with the advent of new technologies in endurance training and sports more generally, there are a number of new ways for athletes to structure their training. These enable more precision in varying training intensities and stress, allowing for better monitoring of the fatigue load on their bodies. Examples include using power data for bike and run training, pace for run training, and more.

PERCEIVED EXERTION

The oldest training method known to man is that which is based on how an athlete feels in the moment of training, using that to guide intensity. It is very effective – the best athletes in the world know they have to rely more on their own bodies and sense of what is right and wrong, than they do on their coach. Their bodies will tell them when they need to back off the intensity, and when they feel good enough to take a risk. This doesn't mean they sprint in the middle of an IRONMAN race, but rather their experience as an athlete helps them know what efforts they can sustain for the long haul.

The most famous and popular scale of effort for perceived exertion comes from Gunnar Borg, 1998. The Borg Scale runs from 6 to 20, where 6 is no exertion at all, and 20 is an absolute maximal effort. The scale is shown in Figure 1.

Most IRONMAN triathlon efforts range from 10 to 15 on the scale early in a race, dependent on athlete's goals. Once an athlete enters the later stages, where they can be extremely fatigued, they may proclaim efforts near 20, despite the speed or pace not being close to an effort representative of that type of intensity.

This is where RPE –[Rated Perceived Exertion (see Figure 1) – can be effective for training, while also providing a challenge. Athletes think IRONMAN efforts should be hard, but hard is relative to the point in the race. If an athlete begins an IRONMAN race at 15-17, they will certainly find those early efforts costly to their performance later in the race.

Most IRONMAN 70.3 triathlon efforts range from 12 to 17 on the Borg Scale. This makes sense given the much shorter duration, comparatively. Of course, what the actual output is depends on the athlete and their goals.

▶ It is important to maintain a measured RPE throughout the entirety of the race, as these athletes are at the 2017 IRONMAN 70.3 Staffordshire, to avoid becoming too fatigued.

HEART RATE

Heart rate monitors were the first portable technology introduced into endurance sport, allowing athletes to help gauge intensity. This prevented overtraining, while enabling more precision in finding the correct intensity and training load. It is still commonly used as a gauge for intensity and as a pacing tool for athletes, both in training and racing.

Heart rate training provides a number of advantages and challenges. Some of the advantages include:

- Great guide for beginner athletes on how to better gauge appropriate intensities for the workouts or races.
- Simple intensity guidance. Need to go harder? Increase the heart rate. Need to go easier? Decrease the heart rate. Very easy!
- Heart rate based efforts generally correspond well with aerobic intensities, if using zones, or just as a governor for not exceeding a certain heart rate during a workout or race.
- Reductions in heart rate for a given output of pace or power can help show a positive adaptation to the output pace or power, even if pace or power have not improved themselves. The heart has shown it doesn't have to work as hard for the same output and effort.

The challenges with training based on heart rate include:

- Heart rate can be skewed, based upon diet, stress, fatigue, excitement or, even, conditions.
- Accurate measurement of threshold heart rate, from which to base training zones for correct intensities, becomes vital. Get the baseline wrong, and other intensities are likely not correct.
- Heart rate intensities are not the same for the different sports: running will have higher heart rates, because of the load bearing efforts required compared to cycling or swimming. Cycling, in turn, is generally higher than swimming. This tends to cause confusion to athletes. If an athlete tries to apply the same heart rate intensities to swimming and cycling as their running, they will likely overdo the training stress, or not be able to achieve the heart rates, and find themselves frustrated with their training.
- There are sport-specific heart rate zones for cycling as well, but again the basis point for threshold heart rate needs to be accurate, or training intensities will be off, leading to over-training or under-training.
- Cycling power zones and running pace zones don't tend to match with heart rate zones for the same sport. For example, it is not uncommon for an athlete to ride at a Zone 2 power, which is an aerobic intensity specific to IRONMAN racing. But this effort might still be in heart rate Zone 1 for cycling. This often confuses and frustrates athletes.
- Last, heart rate has a delayed response time relative to effort and intensity. For example, if an athlete starts a 30-second sprint effort, their heart rate won't achieve its peak until likely after the 30-second sprint is complete. It is not uncommon for athletes to begin an interval and be in the correct heart rate zone early, but exceed it later in the interval. Conversely, an athlete can start an interval below the heart rate target, and think they are not going hard enough, but it is simply a matter of the time taken for the heart rate to level out in order to determine if the intensity is correct.

CYCLING POWER

Power meters for bikes were, for a long time, considered to be a major luxury given their cost, despite the valuable information they provided. Now the prices have greatly reduced and made them more readily available to nearly every athlete who wants to utilize one.

Power meters measure the force applied to the pedal (how hard an athlete pushes on the pedals) and the speed of that force application (the pedal cadence). This provides a work rate, measured in watts, describing how well the body can move itself through space. There are many advantages to this type of measurement for performance in training and racing:

- Because the metric is output based, it is much more accurate than perceived exertion or heart rate in its measurements for athletes.
- Provides simple guidance on bike training

◄ The swim leg is the most difficult to measure performance levels during IRONMAN events. If tracking heart rates, it is important to have an accurate base rate to measure from.

85

intensities. If the watts are too low, increase the effort. If the watts are too high, decrease the effort.

- Athletes using a power meter have a major pacing advantage, knowing they are at an intensity they can sustain, even if heart rate or perceived exertion tell them otherwise.

- Since the output on cycling efforts can be measured, the training stress for the rides can be measured much more specifically. Training stress balance is the key to adaptations and performance, and power meters and their data provide a huge advantage

- An athlete who doesn't have power data can't really measure gains in cycling training very well, as heart rate won't change from session to session, or is too unreliable. Speed as a metric on the bike has too many variables that affect it to measure progress in training; hills, winds, road surface, heat and other riders all affect it. Power is measured in watts, which are unaffected by winds, heart rate or other factors. It is an objective, absolute value that applies to any training session you want to compare.

- A poor pedal stroke is something that can destroy an athlete's performance, fatiguing them faster than normal, and not maximizing the efforts to propel the bike forward. Power data can provide direct, instantaneous feedback to help athletes see how effective they are in applying their forces to the pedals.

- Power data from year to year also provide a measurement of progress for athletes, to see how far they have come, where they made mistakes in their training, and where they had successes.

The only real drawbacks to using power are the costs of purchasing a power meter, and the time it takes to learn to use it effectively. At any IRONMAN event, however, the majority of athletes will be using them, and the higher the goals the athletes have, the more prevalent power meters are. As long as the athlete's threshold power is accurately estimated or measured, power is the best tool for cycling performance there is.

RUN PACE

Many athletes use pace as a metric to not only gauge their training intensities but also to predict their performances. If done conservatively, understanding the pace which one is capable of, instead of what one hopes to run, can be very useful.

Pace zones in training are also useful guides to intensity for athletes preparing to race, but just like heart rate and power zones, they require an accurate run pace threshold to be determined first so that other intensity levels are accurate.

Generally, run pace is a better measurement for performance when coupled for comparison with heart rate, perceived exertion and even run power (see below). If an athlete can't quite see an improvement in pace, they can see if heart rate or perceived exertion for that same pace is improved – these improvements can be excellent for building confidence. Using a specific heart rate to run at, such as the aerobic threshold (the point at which breathing becomes a little labored), and tracking the pace output for those workouts is another great way to utilize both run pace and heart rate data to see the training response and adaptations an athlete is seeking in pursuit of their goals.

RUN POWER

Run power technology is very new, and is positioned to take over the running training world, much like cycling power has done. The complexities of it are too deep to expand on here, but any athlete who is beyond beginner level and higher than simple finisher goals, and who is looking to be more competitive, should consider looking at this technology for their training.

Run power is much more reliable for measuring run training stress than run pace or volume is, which are the common ways athletes and runners measure intensity and training load. Hilly routes can easily make a hard run seem slow, or an easy pace seem hard. There are also a number of insights to biomechanical improvements that run power data can provide, that pace simply can't.

The training plans listed in this book don't include run power, as the plans are focused on beginners or finishers, but as goals increase in their challenge, run power technology and data becomes more critical for achieving them.

▶ Head down and focused: even when cycling through the most challenging terrains, paying attention to cycling power will ensure an athlete does not fatigue too early in the race.

RACE EXECUTION

The best way for athletes to avoid race day mistakes is to have a plan to execute. The more detailed and specific the plan, the more outside variables can be eliminated, and athletes can therefore turn their focus to the controllable variables. This helps keep athletes calm, confident, and focused on the things that will help them to perform their best.

HAVE A PLAN

The best plans begin well before the race starts, and even before race day. Effective race plans begin days before, and continue into race day starting from the time an athlete wakes up to then cover everything until they cross the finish line. Athletes should write out these details in order to make sure they don't overlook anything, and to better commit the preparation process and execution to memory. The race plan should review and highlight the following:

- Travel plans to race location, if far away, and ways to mitigate fatigue from travel
- Checklist of items to pack and prepare for the race
- Race-day plans
    - *Time to wake up*
    - *Breakfast plan*
    - *Departure and arrival times at race venue*
    - *Estimated time to get from parking to transition/bike check-in*
    - *Estimated time to complete bike check-in and prepare transition spot*
    - *Warm-up procedure and timeline for warm-ups to be effective for race*
    - *Swim start positioning and pacing plan*
    - *Swim to bike transition plan*
    - *Bike pacing plan*
    - *Bike nutrition plan*
    - *Bike to run transition plan*
    - *Run pacing plan*
    - *Run nutrition plan*
    - *Potential changes or flexibilities to the plan based on weather conditions*
    - *Contingency plans in case of issues (lost nutrition, crash, flat tire, mechanical)*

If athletes write this plan out, there is a great learning opportunity after the race to go back and review the race execution and compare it to the plan. They can then assess where the plan was effective, and where it needs to be modified for future races.

If athletes take the time to write out a plan for their race, then the race's outcome and what is needed to achieve that outcome become clear and more likely to make it happen.

RACE NUTRITION STRATEGIES

Nutrition is probably the most commonly overlooked aspect of the race. Nutrition is something an athlete must plan for in races that last four hours or longer. There is no athlete who can compete at these events successfully and not consume calories during the race. There just aren't enough stores of calories in the muscle glycogen to support the body at a relatively competitive intensity for the durations of IRONMAN and IRONMAN 70.3 events.

Even though many may think IRONMAN and IRONMAN 70.3 events should be run at aerobic intensities – which should rely on fat reserves – many athletes exceed the aerobic intensity level, which means glycogen stores become crucial. Also, training and preparation, as well as pacing, will affect how much glycogen is needed to race.

If an athlete has higher goals and is racing hard, then the nutrition aspect of the race becomes even harder to get right and increasingly riskier. Intensity increases the sensitivity of the stomach, creating nausea, and decreasing the ability of the stomach to process calories consumed. Many athletes have experienced gastrointestinal distress in races. Nutrition must command the attention of athletes in their training, in terms of calories consumed per hour, as much as work out details do.

In general, the goal is not to eat as much as one can consume during the race, but simply to take in what is needed to accomplish the goal. The more calories an athlete consumes, the more likely the event of gastrointestinal distress, and the less racing or focus on what they should be doing will happen.

As a guideline, most athletes should come into the race fully fueled to begin with. This means hydrating and eating well in the days leading into the race, followed by a breakfast on race morning that should be effective in topping off glycogen stores.

Other nutritional guidelines for racing:

- Athletes should typically not consume more than 250 calories per hour on the bike, and 150 calories per hour on the run. Once they exceed these levels, risk of gastrointestinal distress increases greatly.
- The harder an athlete races, the more their calories should be liquid based for easier digestion.
- Liquid calories don't replace hydration needs, especially in hotter race events. Be sure to hydrate, as it helps with digestion of calories as well.
- Plan the logistics of race nutrition as well as the items themselves. How will the calories be carried and consumed? One bottle? Two bottles? Six bottles? What is the concentration of the calories in a bottle? Will the athlete practice the nutritional strategy at that concentration? How many gels or bars will be consumed? Where they will be stored? What will the aid stations provide?

After reading this section, it is easy to understand why nutrition can be so easily overlooked, and how it is crucial to race performance, and needs to be specifically planned and executed for success.

◀ Nutrition is an easily overlooked aspect of the race-day plan, but the consequences of doing so can be disastrous.

COMMON RACE MISTAKES TO AVOID

Here are some of the most common mistakes athletes make on race day that derail their preparation:

- Trying something new on race day: do not try anything that has not been practiced with, tested or tried in training. This includes nutritional items, clothes and apparel, equipment, and even strategies and warm-ups, pre-race workouts, and more. These can shock the body, make athletes not feel well on race day, derail confidence, cause issues during the race that were unexpected, and more.
- Getting to a race with not enough time: most athletes underestimate the timeline and how quickly things can get off schedule. Athletes who are rushed to get to a start sacrifice a proper warm-up, miss checking the details of things that can derail their race, and more. It's always best to have extra time that is not needed than need more time, especially on race day! An athlete who is rushed is an athlete who is NOT ready to race.
- Poor pacing: there is no nutritional plan or equipment that can make up for poor race-day pacing decisions. Know the paces and intensities you're capable of sustaining. This comes from training effectively.
- Underestimating temperature: Most IRONMAN triathlons start off in the early morning hours. These tend to be the coolest, or even coldest, hours of the day. Yet many athletes will show up to a race underdressed and not prepared for the colder temperatures. Always bring clothes guaranteed to keep you warm and ready for the race. A cold, shivering athlete is an athlete who is NOT ready to race.
- Always bring a wetsuit: athletes tend to think the water will be too warm for wetsuits to be legal when traveling to warm or tropical destinations. There have been numerous athletes who have been surprised to learn a race was wetsuit legal, or the water not as warm as they expected and wanted a wetsuit that they didn't think to bring. Sometimes weather patterns can change dramatically and affect water temperatures much more than expected. Even if a race is fully expected to be non-wetsuit, always bring a wetsuit to a race, even on race morning, just in case things change.

◀ Cycling 112 miles at the best of times is a challenge. Doing so in the heat or with unfamiliar equipment can hinder the race plan enormously. Preparation is of paramount importance.

TIPS FOR BETTER PERFORMANCE

- Whatever athletes tell themselves on the start line is usually the greatest determinant of the race result. Those who are excited to race and express their fitness usually have great races. Those who are unsure, lack excitement, are worried about factors or variables outside of their control, or are consumed with anxiety about the race result, don't tend to race well. If a coach could peek into the minds of athletes on the start line, and hear the things they're saying to themselves, they could likely pick out who is going to perform well and who isn't. Make sure the mind is positive and excited to race on the start line.

- Poor pacing can derail the best training. Most athletes don't truly understand the pace their training has prepared them for. Just because an athlete feels good early in a long race, doesn't mean they should push and take a risk, especially if their training hasn't resembled that risk.

- Planning is the key to making all the training pay off on race day. Without a plan, athletes will be faced with so many variables and situations they can't possibly manage in the moment, or can become distracted as to what is most important for performance at that time. Have a plan, and execute it.

- Race nutrition must be dialed in, tested and tweaked many weeks before race day. If an athlete hasn't proven they can be successful in race specific workouts with their race nutrition, then it will never work on race day.

- The days leading into an IRONMAN race can often be socially demanding with friends, family, events and other things to attend and do. Athletes who perform best tend to be a little selfish as race day approaches, making sure they aren't stretching themselves far, many times choosing to stay in for the evening to relax, get a proper meal, and a good night's sleep. Many athletes have made mistakes of being on their feet all day in the lead-up to a race. Avoid those situations if possible, and relax in comfort in the days leading into a race.

IRONMAN events are big investments of time in training, and on race day. Great race results begin with proper preparation, a solid understanding of how to train, avoiding overtraining, and showing up to the start line with a plan to execute, and a mindset that is excited to race. These are the efforts that will yield great performances, and where an athlete's focus should be.

The training plans later in this chapter will help guide beginners who are looking to finish their first IRONMAN triathlon.

▶ As race day dawns, the many hours of training will feel incredibly worthwhile.

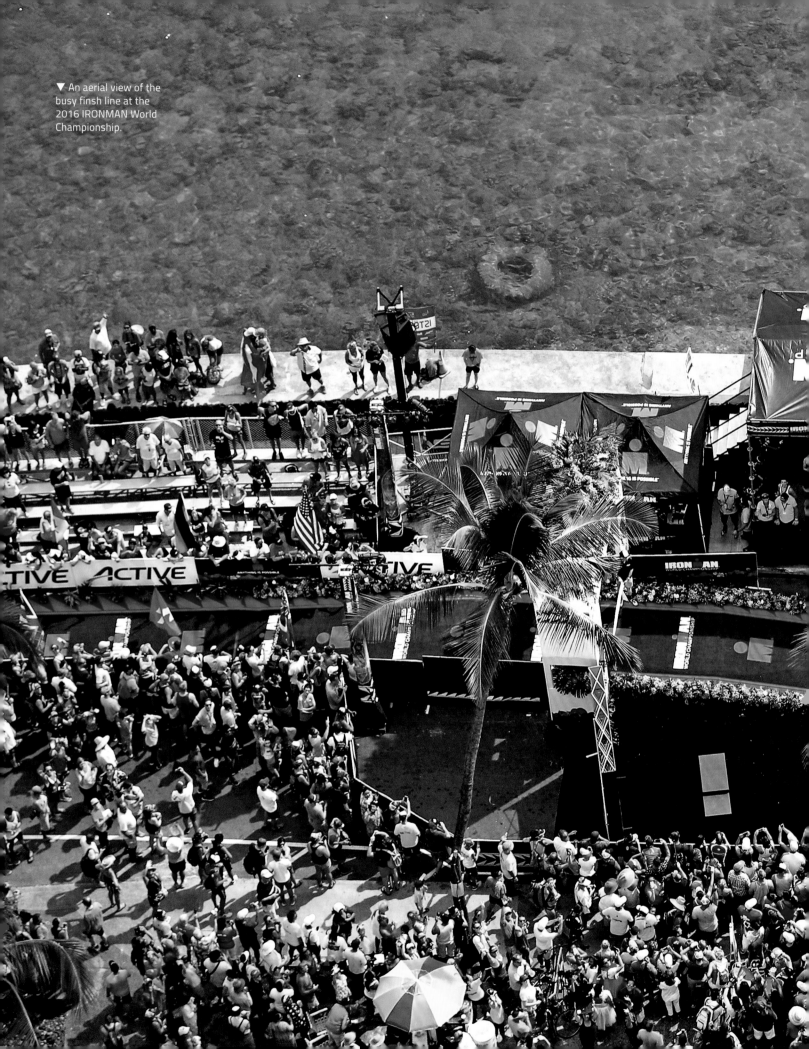

▼ An aerial view of the busy finsh line at the 2016 IRONMAN World Championship.

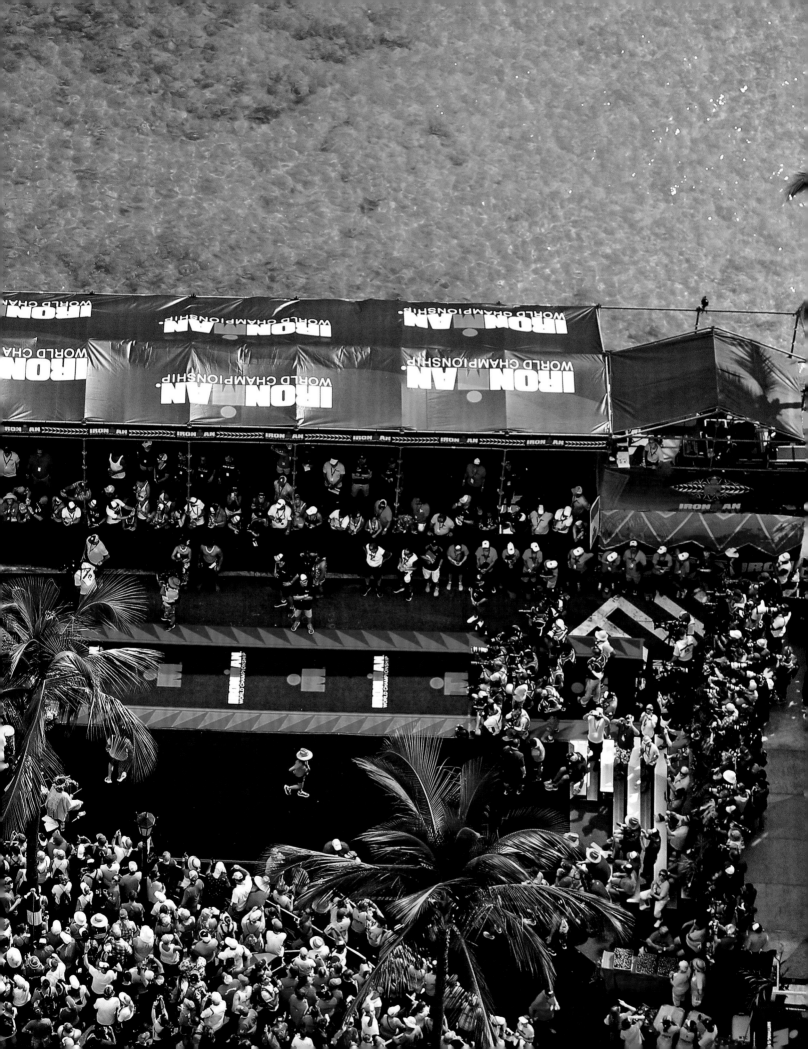

ALL IN THE MIND

Self-doubt can be an athlete's own worst enemy when it comes to preparing for and completing an IRONMAN race. Paddy Cloete, a psychologist, as well as an IRONMAN athlete in his own right, has been clear about the importance of mental attitude in triathlon:

"We all have conversations with ourselves," he writes. *"Every athlete hears two competing voices – a negative critic and a positive cheerleader. The negative critic encourages you to focus on what could go wrong and on what not to do. Your critic makes you dwell on your past mistakes and encourages you to compete with the mindset of avoiding making mistakes. If you listen to your critic, you allow your fears to get in the way of your dreams. You focus on what you cannot do which in turn interferes with what you can do. This destroys your confidence, which is reflected in your performance."*

The critic can be with any athlete from the very beginning, alongside them even as they lower themselves into the water for the swim. It might make them worry, for example, about the size of the waves and the likelihood of not being able to get behind them. If this voice is allowed to dominate, it becomes far more likely that the athletes will find themselves stuck in the break of the waves, not moving forward. But there is another voice, a cheerleader and powerful ally, which can reinforce positive thought. This is the voice that encourages those same athletes to focus on the fact that they can swim and that just because the conditions might be scary or unfamiliar, it does not mean that they have lost their abilities. According to Cloete, it is this voice that focuses the mind behind the break of the waves and that cheers the athletes on to keep moving. He believes both voices – the critic and the cheerleader – are always present and competing for attention. This theory has been proven by practitioners of mindfulness in many different situations. The more the cheerleading voice is listened to, the quieter the critic will become – and thus, the more successful the athlete will be.

Cloete writes:

"Arnold Palmer, one of the most successful golfers of all times, kept the following saying in his locker to remind him of this important truth: 'If you think you are beaten, you are. If you think you dare not, you don't. If you'd like to win, but you think you can't, it is almost certain you won't. If you think you'll lose, you've lost. For, out in the world, you'll find success begins with a fellow's will. It's all a state of the mind. Life's battles don't always go to the stronger or faster man; but sooner or later the man who wins is the man who thinks he can.'"

It is important to remember that the two voices coexist, both in life and in triathlon, and athletes must choose for themselves which voice they will listen to. This is particularly true when embarking on a challenge as large as an IRONMAN event. Positive thinking does not always ensure a positive outcome, but negative thinking almost always ensures a disappointing outcome. "It is best to always turn your cheerleader up to full volume and mute your critic!" writes Cloete.

▶ An aerial view of the 2017 IRONMAN World Championship. On race day it is of vital importance to keep calm and positive in the crowded opening leg of the event.

> ## "Positive thoughts translate into positive actions. Actions become habits. Habits become character. Character becomes destiny."
>
> ## PADDY CLOETE, PSYCHOLOGIST AND IRONMAN COMPETITOR

KEEPING IT IN THE IRONMAN FAMILY

Many IRONMAN athletes have busy family lives, and there is no reason for family life to suffer when preparing for a race. In fact, many athletes find that their family members are keen to help in any way possible – whether that involves keeping them company during hours spent in the pool or on the road or providing transportation to and from races. Families will find that they are always welcomed at IRONMAN events. Often, athletes incorporate IRONMAN events into existing family vacations. The race itself might be the main purpose for the journey, but finding an event located in an area surrounded by family-friendly activities can be key for ensuring that everyone has fun.

IRONMAN race locations all over the world offer much more than just a race experience. Athletes with a penchant for theme parks might choose to participate in the IRONMAN 70.3® Florida event, for example. The Global IRONMAN and IRONMAN 70.3 Events chapter has further details of available races, but for a full range of choices the IRONMAN website is an invaluable resource. When scheduling a family vacation around an IRONMAN race, it is important to ensure the right balance between preparing for the event and spending time together. The majority of the trip can be enjoyed normally, but it is of the utmost importance to include at least one quiet day immediately before the race itself, otherwise the many months of training could go to waste.

Fortunately, even the IRONMAN events can include something for all members of the family. Where available, those under the age of 18 can run in IRONKIDS® races and many weekends include other events alongside IRONMAN or IRONMAN 70.3 races. The atmosphere at these events is fun and family members will find that being loyal and loud supporters is gratifying, too. As part of a pre-race ritual, many athletes scope out each leg of the course; doing this with the family is a great way to plan out perfect spectating spots.

Different spectators have different needs. For some, the only consideration is which area is best to watch the race; but for others, nearby amenities such as playgrounds, seating, restrooms, or food and drink are important factors. Adult members of the family who want to be involved can sign up as volunteers. The most vital role for spectating families is to wave and cheer as the athletes pass.

▶ Shirin Gerami celebrating with her mother after her boundary-breaking performance in 2016.

▼Craig Alexander with his daughter Lucy after winning the IRONMAN Asia-Pacific Championship in 2012. Finishing an IRONMAN event is made all the sweeter if it can be shared with family and friends.

QUALIFYING SLOTS

Every IRONMAN event offers a minimum of one qualifying slot per age group for the IRONMAN World Championship. Which race is the easiest? As the years go by and the IRONMAN global series matures, that question becomes harder to answer. Not only do race-day conditions change year to year, but age-group racing is also becoming more and more competitive. The number of slots in each category is dependent on the number of athletes in each of the age groups – typically, in an IRONMAN race, the 35–39 and 40–44 age groups have the most competitors and the most slots – so it is not necessary to win the age group to secure a spot at Kona.

LEGACY PROGRAMS

The Legacy Program grants loyal athletes an opportunity to compete in the IRONMAN World Championship at least once in their lifetime. To be eligible for selection, athletes must have completed a minimum of 12 full-distance IRONMAN races, never started an IRONMAN World Championship race, completed at least one full-distance IRONMAN event in each of the preceding two years, and registered for an IRONMAN event in the current year.

AUCTION

Every April, a number of slots are auctioned, with IRONMAN approval, on eBay, with all of the proceeds going to The IRONMAN Foundation, Inc. The auction takes place over a number of weeks with one slot available per week. However, places at the auction do not come cheap, as each slot begins with a minimum bid of USD $10,000.

HANDCYCLE (HC)

Athletes who are paraplegic, quadriplegic or double above-the-knee amputees and use a hand-cranked cycle on the bike segment and a racing chair for the run segment, may compete for IRONMAN World Championship qualifying slots. The IRONMAN website is a valuable resource to see which races offer these slots.

▼ Bill Bell at the 2001 IRONMAN World Championship, shortly after he had broken the record to become the oldest IRONMAN finisher at the age of 78.

"I did my first IRONMAN in February '82 and never looked back."

BILL BELL, WHO FINISHED 32 IRONMAN EVENTS, WITH HIS FINAL ONE AT THE AGE OF 78

▶ Italian Alex Zanardi, a former F1 driver and Paralympic champion, completed the 2014 IRONMAN World Championship in an incredible time of 9:47:14.

"Before the race – before every race I ever do – I write on my race wristband 'Never ever give up' ... try and remain confident. I realize again the power of the human spirit."

CHRISSIE WELLINGTON, FOUR-TIME IRONMAN WORLD CHAMPION

MILITARY

Amateur active duty military personnel, regardless of country, gender, or branch of service, whether Navy, Air Force, Marines, Coast Guard, or Military Police in countries that delineate their military police force on equal status as their active-duty military service, can compete for available slots. Veterans, reservists, retirees, and National Guard personnel are not eligible to compete in the Military division. Participants must present a valid government-issued military identification card at athlete check-in at each of the qualifying races and the IRONMAN World Championship itself. The IRONMAN website provides further details on the qualifying criteria for the IRONMAN World Championship Military Division.

VOLUNTEERS

Another way to get involved with IRONMAN requires no training at all and yet, it is a vital part of every race. Volunteers help with almost all aspects; including at aid stations, in construction, in medical facilities, with security, on the bike course, in transition areas, at registration, on the finish line, in post-race supplies, at credentials checks, in information and at the warehouse. Experienced volunteers with a talent for organization and good social skills, not to mention a true love for the event, can be captains who help coordinate volunteer teams to be efficient and successful.

The duties on the actual day of the race are vast. Volunteers distribute food and beverages at aid stations; carry supplies; fill, hand out and pick up water bottles; operate radios and telephones; hand out sponges; assist in getting equipment out to transition areas; massage the athletes and much more. Many doctors, nurses and paramedics from all over the world also donate their time to staff critical medical facilities. The volunteers are at the very core of what IRONMAN represents – they are a prized group of people who give their time and talents to help others achieve life-changing goals.

▲ Volunteers at the 2017 IRONMAN World Championship helping the athletes re-fuel.

▶ Jan Frodeno gets well and truly soaked during the 2016 IRONMAN World Championship by some enthusiastic volunteers.

THE FIRST TIME

For those who need a little extra incentive to get going, hearing stories from IRONMAN athletes can provide the inspiration needed to get started. Below, a selection of athletes reflect on the reasons behind their own personal journeys to the finish line.

"When I was little I watched the IRONMAN World Championship on TV," recalls Joe Huy, a Californian aviation consultant and 13-time IRONMAN finisher. "I knew someday I wanted to race in Kona, to test myself and see what I was made of. In 2000, IRONMAN California was announced, and I knew I couldn't pass it up, this was my chance. The challenge of preparing for the unknown was addictive and required a target focus mentality that I found very appealing. I have been hooked ever since."

Businessman Craig Stevens, from Missouri, had completed 14 events when he told IRONMAN, "I had done IRONMAN 70.3 races before and then got out of triathlon for five years. Nothing motivates a person more than knowing you are signed up for an IRONMAN event, because there is so much prep that needs to be done just to finish. I actually had a decent race!"

"Thinking back to my first IRONMAN triathlon in 2004," explained Nicki Davies, a first-aid officer and college student administrator in Melbourne, Australia, "What made me think I can do this was the year before my husband Alan did his first IRONMAN race and as I watched the day unfold I started to think, 'I could do this.' After he finished, I told him we have to stay and watch all the competitors finish. I can't explain the emotions or how proud I felt for them all. I wanted to be one of them, I wanted Mike Reilly to call me across the finish line and hear, 'Nicki! You are an IRONMAN!'" Davies has since completed 14 IRONMAN events.

Another finisher of 14 events is Douglas Eichhorn, of Maryland. "I signed up for my first triathlon, which was IRONMAN 70.3 Florida, and IRONMAN UK on the same day," said Eichhorn, a self-employed home improvement contractor. "It was on November 17, 2006, when I woke up an overweight alcoholic with no hopes or dreams and convinced that I was going to die. I decided at that moment to do the hardest thing I'd ever heard of... IRONMAN! Today, I believe that my dedication to IRONMAN has not only saved my life, but it has also given me a life."

"I attended the IRONMAN Wisconsin race and spectated along with some friends and family and was completely blown away by the event," said Kristin Wedemeyer, a 13-time finisher from Virginia. "I was inspired to see all kinds of people participating. Witnessing their grit, determination, and relentless drive to finish was just amazing! I returned home and signed up for the 2006 IRONMAN Lake Placid event through a charity spot, and I said I was 'one and done.' Clearly, that wasn't the case and during the race I realized how much I loved both training for and racing IRONMAN."

Rachel Balding is an event coordinator from Melbourne. She had finished 13 IRONMAN events when she was asked to think back to her favorite one. "In 1994, I watched on television as Greg Welch ran down the finish chute of the IRONMAN World Championship in Hawai`i and from that moment on it has been my goal to run down the finish chute in Kona. This is what got me started and what keeps me going."

▶ The joyful feeling of finishing: no matter whether it is an athlete's first or fiftieth IRONMAN event, being cheered on by the crowd while crossing the finish line is an unforgettable moment.

Advancing years shouldn't discourage anyone from becoming an IRONMAN athlete. A motivating example of this can be found in Simon Butterworth, who was 70 years old in 2017 and didn't start getting into triathlon until his mid-40s. He has now finished 13 IRONMAN World Championships. The IRONMAN veteran grew up in the seaside town of Tramore in Ireland, where his summers were spent cycling to swim spots. He was a youth track and field champion and played cricket and rugby as well as fencing.

Butterworth started running to combat his middle-age weight gain. "I didn't like the trend line," he said. Then someone suggested he go and watch a triathlon: he immediately liked what he saw, deeming the crew "a fun bunch." Back in Ireland, Butterworth ran his first 10K and lost to his brother-in-law. "He got to the finish in time to buy me a Guinness and was standing in the door of the pub smiling with a pint in each hand when I crossed the line."

Three years later, Butterworth purchased his first second-hand bike and raced his first triathlon in 1992. "I was surprised to find I should have taken up cycling before. I had the fastest bike split in my age group and finished fourth. I was hooked. Triathlon was the way to hold onto my youth as best I could."

Demonstrating that anyone can participate, by 2017, Butterworth had finished more than 130 triathlons, including 22 IRONMAN races, more than 30 IRONMAN 70.3 races, and four ITU World Championships. He failed to finish only once.

▶ Simon Butterworth on board his bike at IRONMAN Boulder.

▼ British athlete Alistair Brownlee celebrates winning the IRONMAN 70.3 Dubai in 2018 – all the training paid off.

"Do the training you love, remind yourself why you do it and hopefully it will all come good for you."
ALISTAIR BROWNLEE, OLYMPIC GOLD MEDALIST AND IRONMAN ATHLETE

▲ Christian Haupt of Germany impressively shows he is still fresh and energetic at the finish of the IRONMAN World Championship in 2017.

the others on the podium, too. I had forgotten what I have told so many of the athletes I have coached, that a strong bike, paced correctly, will allow a strong run."

Butterworth appreciates his good fortune in all aspects of his life. "I'm lucky to have found the sport in which I can excel," he said, "and to have a very special woman in my life who has put up with my antics. And I'm lucky for the great genes from my Scottish and Viking ancestors." Like a true warrior, he plans to keep racing until the day he cannot physically do it anymore. "I found a perfect bumper sticker for our van that said, 'There will come a day when I can no longer race IRONMAN. Today is not that day.'"

People have overcome all sorts of difficulties to participate in an IRONMAN race. Former drug addict and alcoholic Todd Crandell swapped his addictions for more than 27 IRONMAN races and 37 IRONMAN 70.3 races. His problems began very early in life when his mother committed suicide. He attempted to fill the void left by her death with alcohol and drugs. "The moment I tried cocaine, I thought instantly, 'That's it, that's what I've been looking for,'" he told IRONMAN. His cocaine use was prolific by the time he was in high school, where he had become a promising ice hockey player. He was caught using the drug on the bus to a game and was subsequently kicked off the team. In 1993, he became sober and, in the process of getting his life back, discovered triathlon. He finished his first IRONMAN race in 1999 and hasn't stopped racing since.

Of course, not everyone who becomes an IRONMAN athlete does so because of life-changing events. For many, it is simply a desire to become fit and healthy, and IRONMAN events provide the perfect motivation to achieve this goal. When Bob McKeown, a primary-school teacher from New York, struggled to catch his breath after climbing a flight of stairs with his students, he knew it was time for a change. He quickly progressed from running during his lunch break to taking part in road racing before moving on to competing in duathlons. He then asked himself, "What should a lifelong surfer-turned-runner/cyclist do next?" He found the answer in triathlon. "I have never been bored a day in my life after adopting the lifestyle of training for triathlons." McKeown eventually received his coaching certification and started his own coaching business.

The IRONMAN World Championship that made Butterworth feel like a true IRONMAN athlete came in 2006. After suffering a broken derailleur, he managed to keep going on a borrowed bike. "I finished with all those amazing people who endure hours running in the darkness. I had some very special conversations that night on the way to a 15:30 finish. I really got it that night that just finishing makes you an IRONMAN – where you finished was unimportant." On his 13th start at the IRONMAN World Championship, he found his magic moment, winning the 70–74 age group by over an hour. "I knew I had my best chance of finally winning," he said. "I had some very strong runners in my age group, but my stats suggested I had the best swim/bike combination. Much to my surprise, I found out afterwards that I had the fastest run split of

"I didn't have cycling shorts at that time, so the night before I cut off a pair of blue jeans so I'd have pockets to stick money in, meaning I could make my stops at our informal aid stations – ha ha! – which turned out to be gas stations, food stores and McDonald's!"

DAVE ORLOWSKI, THIRD PLACE IN THE FIRST-EVER IRONMAN, 1978

Over the past decade, McKeown has finished numerous IRONMAN events but, like so many others, always wanted to race at the IRONMAN World Championship in Kailua-Kona, Hawai`i. He got there eventually by obtaining a charity spot through the IRONMAN Foundation and raised money to support the Foundation's community grants. Raising enough money for a charity slot can be difficult alongside all the physical training, but McKeown thought creatively. He not only hosted a 600-person pub crawl sponsored by local restaurants, he also promoted online donations in which he encouraged people to sponsor each mile of his next 140.6-mile race.

As McKeown, and many of the other contributors in this chapter, have shown, there are many routes to competing in IRONMAN events and many reasons to get there. But for every single person who takes part, in all different areas – whether it is competing, organizing, volunteering or simply supporting the IRONMAN athletes as they give it their all on the course – the ethos hasn't changed in all the years since Hawai`i first witnessed an IRONMAN race: when you put your mind to it, ANYTHING IS POSSIBLE™.

▶ Dave Orlowski with his borrowed Sears Free Spirit bicycle and "cycling shorts" in 1978.

16-WEEK IRONMAN TRAINING

	DAY 1	DAY 2	DAY 3	DAY 4	DAY 5	DAY 6	DAY 7
WEEK 1	**40 min easy run:** 4 min run, 1 min walk. Repeat	**30 min swim:** 5 min WU and CD, 20 min steady swim **45 min CV bike:** easy to mod	**30 min swim:** 5 min WU and CD, 20 min steady swim **40 min easy run:** 4 min run, 1 min walk. Repeat	Recovery Day	**150 min bike:** easy to mod rolling hills, seated **15 min easy run:** transition run	**30 min swim:** 5 min WU and CD **40 min easy run:** 4 min run, 1 min walk. Repeat **60 min easy bike**	Recovery Day
WEEK 2	**40 min easy run:** 4 min run, 1 min walk. Repeat **2700m swim:** 450m WU+CD. 6x150m, 6x100m, 6x50m	**60 min bike:** trainer: 3x5 min SL WU+CD. 3x10 min easy to mod	**3000m build swim:** 6x75m WU+CD. 3x100m, 2x200m, 2x300m, 2x400m **60 min easy run:** 4 min run, 1 min walk. Repeat	**30 min swim:** 5 min WU and CD, 20 min steady swim	**180 min bike:** easy to mod rolling hills, seated **15 min easy run:** transition run	**60 min easy run:** 4 min run, 1 min walk. Repeat **30 min swim:** open water, steady **60 min CV bike:** easy to mod	Recovery Day
WEEK 3	**3300m build swim:** 300m WU+CD. 12x150m, 3x200m **40 min easy run:** 4 min run, 1 min walk. Repeat	**90 min easy run:** 4 min run, 1 min walk. Repeat	**60 min mod bike:** trainer: 3x5 min SL WU+CD. 3x10 min **2600m build swim:** 100, 2x200 WU+CD. 4x150, 4x50, 4x100, 4x75, 2x200	**3100m desc swim:** 2x300m WU. 8x150m, 8x100m, 8x50m. 100m CD	**180 min bike:** easy to mod rolling hills, seated **15 min easy run:** transition run	**30 min swim:** open water, steady **60 min easy run:** 4 min run, 1 min walk. Repeat **90 min CV bike:** easy to mod	Recovery Day
WEEK 4	**4000m test swim:** 800m + 4x25m WU. 5x400m test set. 1000m CD **60 min easy run:** 4 min run, 1 min walk. Repeat	**60 min bike:** trainer: 3x5 min SL WU+CD. 3x10 min steady	**2500m swim:** 500 WU. 4X200, 150, 50, 600 pull, 16x25 desc. 200 CD **60 min easy run:** 4 min run, 1 min walk. Repeat	Recovery Day	**180 min bike:** easy to mod rolling hills, seated **15 min easy run:** transition run	**30 min swim:** open water, steady **90 min easy run:** 4 min run, 1 min walk. Repeat	Recovery Day
WEEK 5	**2900m swim:** 6x75 WU+CD. 500, 400, 300, 200, 2x300 **60 min bike:** trainer: 3x5 min SL WU+CD. 3x10 min	**105 min easy run:** 4 min run, 1 min walk. Repeat	**3450m swim:** 500, 6x75 WU. 8x50 desc., 4x75, 6x200, 16x25 build. 200 CD **70 min mod bike:** 15 min WU. 8x4 min S+S. 23 min CD	**30 min swim:** 5 min easy, 20 min steady, 5 min very easy	**240 min bike:** 30 min easy, 210 min mod **15 min easy run:** transition run	**45 min swim:** open water, steady **60 min mod run:** 5 min run, 1 min walk. Repeat **60 min CV bike:** easy to mod	Recovery Day
WEEK 6	**2500m mod swim:** 2x200, 4x25 WU. 2x250, 4x50, 2x200, 4x50, 2x150, 200. 200 CD **70 min mod bike:** 15 min WU. 8x4 min S+S. 23 min CD	**120 min easy run:** 4 min run, 1 min walk. Repeat	**55 min bike:** trainer: 2x20 min, 2x2 min recovery. 11 min CD **2650m swim:** 600m WU. 9x150m, 2x200m, mod to fast. 100m CD	**2450m 3-2-1 swim:** 450 WU. 300, 200, 100, 50 mod. Repeat fast. 7x100 pull **40 min easy run:** 4 min run, 1 min walk. Repeat	**300 min bike:** 30 min easy, 270 min mod **15 min easy run:** transition run	**60 min easy run:** 9 min run, 1 min walk. Repeat **90 min CV bike:** easy to mod **45 min swim:** open water, steady	Recovery Day
WEEK 7	**3000m swim:** 400m WU. 8x200m as 50 fast 100 easy, 16x50m. 200m CD **75 min bike:** trainer: 3x5 min SL WU+CD. 3x15 min steady	**120 min easy run:** 4 min run, 1 min walk. Repeat	**3600m build swim:** 200m WU+CD. 20x25 build. 3x400, 3x200 fast. **55 min mod bike:** trainer: 2x20 min, 2 min RI. 11 min CD	**30 min swim:** 5 min easy WU+CD. 20 min steady mod **40 min easy run:** 4 min run, 1 min walk. Repeat	**360 min bike:** 30 min easy, 330 min mod **30 min easy run:** transition run, 4 min run, 1 min walk. Repeat	**45 min swim:** open water, steady **60 min mod run:** 6 min run, 1 min walk. Repeat **90 min CV bike:** easy to mod	Recovery Day
WEEK 8	**4000m test swim:** 800m + 4x25m WU. 5x400m test set. 1000m CD **5k fast run:** Tempo time trial. 15 min WU. 5k fast	**75 min mod bike:** trainer: 3x20 min, 2 min RI. 11 min CD	**3000m swim:** 600, 4x75 WU. 4x100, 1x800 fast, 6x100 desc. 6x50 CD **90 min easy run:** 4 min run, 1 min walk. Repeat	**30 min swim:** 5 min easy WU+CD. 20 min steady mod	**180 min bike:** easy to mod rolling hills, seated **15 min easy run:** transition run	**45 min swim:** open water, steady **40 min mod run:** 4 min run, 1 min walk. Repeat **60 min CV bike:** easy to mod	Recovery Day

Key: build swim = increase pace throughout workout; CD = cool-down; CV = cadence variance, varying pace throughout; m = metre; desc swim = swim in which each interval is faster than the last; env run = envelope run focussing on technique not effort; min = minute;

PLAN

	DAY 1	DAY 2	DAY 3	DAY 4	DAY 5	DAY 6	DAY 7
WEEK 9	**2900m swim:** 400m, 8x50m WU. 2x500m, 2x250m, 5x100m. 100m CD **40 min run:** 10 min WU+CD. 20 sec fast, 40 easy	**120 min env run:** Easy up to fast pace. Focus on technique	**3200m mod swim:** 300, 200, 100, 12x25 4x(300 mod, 2x75 fast), 400. 100 CD **75 min mod bike:** trainer: 3x20 min, 2 min RI. 11 min CD	**30 min mod swim:** 5 min easy WU+CD. 20 min steady	**360 min bike:** 30 min easy, 330 min mod **30 min easy run:** transition run, 4 min run, 1 min walk. Repeat	**180 min bike:** easy to mod rolling hills, seated **15 min easy run:** transition run	Recovery Day
WEEK 10	**2800m desc swim:** 10x50m, 300m pull WU. 8x100m pull, 400m, 8x50m pull, 200m. 200m CD **50 min easy run:** 4 min run, 1 min walk. Repeat	**135 min env run:** Easy up to fast pace. Focus on technique	**2800m swim:** 800 WU. 4x(50 SA, 100), 3x(25 easy, 75 fast, 300 mod). 200 CD **75 min mod bike:** trainer: 3x20 min, 2 min RI. 11 min CD	**30 min mod swim:** 5 min easy WU+CD. 20 min steady	**360 min bike:** 30 min easy, 330 min mod **30 min easy run:** transition run, 4 min run, 1 min walk. Repeat	**240 min mod bike:** flat to gently rolling course	Recovery Day
WEEK 11	**3100m desc swim:** 600m WU. 8x150m pull, 8x100m pull, 8x50m pull. 100m CD **50 min easy run:** 7 min run, 1 min walk. Repeat	**150 min env run:** Easy up to fast pace. Focus on technique	**4500m fast swim:** 300m WU+CD. 4x25m, 8x75m, 3x400m, 3x300m, 3x200m, 5x100m **75 min mod bike:** trainer: 3x20 min, 2 min RI. 11 min CD	**30 min mod swim:** 5 min easy WU+CD. 20 min steady	**360 min bike:** 30 min easy, 330 min mod **30 min easy run:** transition run, 4 min run, 1 min walk. Repeat	**45 min swim:** open water, steady **240 min mod bike:** flat to gently rolling course	Recovery Day
WEEK 12	**4000m test swim:** 800m + 4x25m WU. 5x400m test set. 1000m CD **60 min easy run:** 9 min run, 1 min walk. Repeat	**86 min mod bike:** trainer: 4x20 min, 2 min RI	**2500m swim:** 500m WU. 4x200m, 150m, 50m, 600m pull, 16x25m desc. 200m CD **90 min easy run:** 5 min run, 1 min walk. Repeat	Recovery Day	**300 min bike:** 30 min easy, 270 min mod **30 min easy run:** transition run, 4 min run, 1 min walk. Repeat	**45 min swim:** open water, steady **120 min env run:** Easy to fast pace. Focus on technique **60 min CV bike:** easy to mod	Recovery Day
WEEK 13	**4400m swim:** 400, 300 pull, 200 WU. 4x(400, 200), 2x400. 300 CD **86 min mod bike:** trainer: 4x20 min, 2 min RI	**60 min env run:** Easy up to fast pace. Focus on technique	**60 min CV bike:** easy to mod **2900m desc swim:** 800m WU. 3x300m, 3x200m, 5x100m. 100m CD	**30 min mod swim:** 5 min easy WU+CD. 20 min steady	**360 min bike:** 30 min easy, 330 min mod **15 min easy run:** transition run	**150 min easy run:** 9 min run, 1 min walk. Repeat **120 min easy bike:** Shortly after run	Recovery Day
WEEK 14	**2700m swim:** 10x50, 300 pull WU. 2x400, 2x300, 2x200. 100 CD **86 min mod bike:** trainer: 4x20 min, 2 min RI	**60 min env run:** Easy up to fast pace. Focus on technique	**60 min CV bike:** easy to mod **2500m desc swim:** 2x300m WU. 6x150m pull, 6x100m pull, 6x50m pull. 100m CD	**50 min mod swim:** 5 min easy WU+CD. 40 min steady	**240 min bike:** 30 min easy, 210 min mod **15 min easy run:** transition run	**380 min easy run:** 12 min run, 3 min walk. Repeat **60 min CV bike:** easy to mod	Recovery Day
WEEK 15	**4000m test swim:** 800m + 4x25m WU. 5x400m test set. 1000m CD **5k fast run:** Tempo time trial. 15 min WU. 5k fast	**86 min mod bike:** trainer: 4x20 min, 2 min RI	**3400m swim:** 2x300, 200 WU. 4x300, 2x200, 1x300, 10x50. 200 CD **60 min env run:** Easy to fast pace. Focus on technique	Recovery Day **Race Plan:** Write out plan, starting from wake up; include schedule, nutrition, pacing	**180 min bike:** 30 min easy, 150 min mod **15 min easy run:** transition run	**3400m swim:** 3000 steady - every 100m go fast for 25m. 400 CD. **60 min CV bike:** easy to mod	Recovery Day
WEEK 16	**2800m swim:** 600, 300 pull, 400, 200 pull WU. 5x200 desc. 300 CD **45 min env run:** Easy to fast pace. Focus on technique	**90 min mod bike:** trainer: 4x20 min, 2 min RI. 4 min CD	Recovery Day	**2100m swim:** 10x50m, 300m pull WU. 2x300m, 2x200m, 2x100m. 100 CD **40 min easy run:** 4 min run, 1 min walk. Repeat	Recovery Day	**Pre-race brick:** 20 min swim, 30 min bike, 15 min run; 2-3 race efforts on each, preferably on race course	**RACE DAY** Good luck!

mod = moderate; pull = use pull buoy or paddles; RI = recovery interval; S+S = stand and sit; SA = swimming with single-arm; SL = pedaling with single-leg; trainer = stationary bike; transition run = easy run immediately after bike; test swim = swim at race pace; WU = warm-up.

16-WEEK IRONMAN 70.3

	DAY 1	DAY 2	DAY 3	DAY 4	DAY 5	DAY 6	DAY 7
WEEK 1	**40 min easy run:** 4 min run, 1 min walk. Repeat	**30 min swim:** 5 min easy, 20 min steady, 5 min very easy **60 min CV bike:** easy to mod	**30 min swim:** 5 min easy, 20 min steady, 5 min very easy **40 min easy run:** 4 min run, 1 min walk. Repeat	Recovery Day	**90 min bike:** easy to mod rolling hills, stay seated **15 min easy run:** transition run	**30 min swim:** 5 min WU and CD **40 min easy run:** 4 min run, 1 min walk. Repeat **60 min easy bike**	Recovery Day
WEEK 2	**40 min easy run:** 4 min run, 1 min walk. Repeat **2700m desc swim:** 600m WU. 6x150m, 6x100m, 6x50m. 300 CD	**50 min bike:** trainer: 3x5 min SL WU+CD. 2x10 min easy to mod	**3000m build swim:** 6x75m WU+CD. 3x100m, 2x200m, 2x300m, 2x400m **40 min easy run:** 4 min run, 1 min walk. Repeat	Recovery Day	**150 min bike:** easy to mod rolling hills, seated **15 min easy run:** transition run	**60 min easy run:** 4 min run, 1 min walk. Repeat **30 min swim:** open water, steady **60 min CV bike:** easy to mod	Recovery Day
WEEK 3	**3300m build swim:** 300m WU+CD. 12x150m, 3x200m **40 min easy run:** 4 min run, 1 min walk. Repeat	**50 min bike:** trainer: 3x5 min SL WU+CD. 2x10 min easy to mod	**2600m build swim:** 100, 2x200 WU+CD. 4x150, 4x50, 4x100, 4x75, 2x200 **60 min easy run:** 4 min run, 1 min walk. Repeat	**3100m desc swim:** 2x300m WU. 8x150m, 8x100m, 8x50m. 100m CD	**120 min bike:** easy to mod rolling hills, seated **15 min easy run:** transition run	**30 min swim:** open water, steady **60 min easy run:** 4 min run, 1 min walk. Repeat **90 min CV bike:** easy to mod	Recovery Day
WEEK 4	**4000m test swim:** 800m + 4x25m WU. 5x400m test set. 1000m CD **40 min easy run:** 4 min run, 1 min walk. Repeat	**60 min bike:** trainer: 3x5 min SL WU+CD. 3x10 min easy to mod	**2500m swim:** 500 WU. 4X200, 150, 50, 600 pull, 16x25 desc. 200 CD **60 min easy run:** 4 min run, 1 min walk. Repeat	Recovery Day	**120 min bike:** easy to mod rolling hills, seated **15 min easy run:** transition run	**30 min swim:** open water, steady **90 min easy run:** 4 min run, 1 min walk. Repeat	Recovery Day
WEEK 5	**2900m swim:** 6x75 WU+CD. 500, 400, 300, 200, 2x300 **60 min bike:** trainer: 3x5 min SL WU+CD. 3x10 min	**90 min easy run:** 4 min run, 1 min walk. Repeat	**70 min mod bike:** 15 min WU. 8x4 min S+S. 23 min CD **3450m swim:** 500, 6x75 WU. 8x50 desc, 4x75, 6x200, 16x25 build. 200 CD	**30 min swim:** 5 min easy, 20 min steady, 5 min very easy	**120 min bike:** 30 min easy, 90 min mod **15 min easy run:** transition run	**45 min swim:** open water, steady **60 min mod run:** 5 min run, 1 min walk. Repeat	Recovery Day
WEEK 6	**2500m mod swim:** 2x200, 4x25 WU. 2x250, 4x50, 2x200, 4x50, 2x150, 200. 200 CD **70 min mod bike:** 15 min WU. 8x4 min S+S. 23 min CD	**105 min easy run:** 4 min run, 1 min walk. Repeat	**55 min bike:** trainer: 2x20 min, 2x2 min recovery. 11 min CD **2650m swim:** 600m WU. 9x150m, 2x200m, mod to fast. 100m CD	**2550m 3-2-1 swim:** 600 WU. 300, 200, 100, 200, mod 100. 50 fast. 200, 100, 6x100 pull. 100 CD	**150 min bike:** 30 min easy, 120 min mod **30 min easy run:** transition run, 4 min run, 1 min walk. Repeat	**60 min easy run:** 9 min run, 1 min walk. Repeat **45 min swim:** open water, steady **60 min CV bike:** easy to mod	Recovery Day
WEEK 7	**3000m swim:** 400m WU. 8x200m as 50 fast 100 easy, 16x50m. 200m CD **75 min bike:** trainer: 3x5 min SL WU+CD. 3x15 min steady	**105 min easy run:** 4 min run, 1 min walk. Repeat	**3600m build swim:** 200m WU+CD. 20x25 build. 6x100, 6x50, 3x(400, 200) **55 min mod bike:** trainer: 2x20 min, 2 min RI. 11 min CD	**30 min swim:** 5 min easy, 20 min steady, 5 min very easy	**150 min bike:** 30 min easy, 120 min mod **30 min easy run:** transition run, 4 min run, 1 min walk. Repeat	**30 min swim:** open water, steady **60 min mod run:** 6 min run, 1 min walk. Repeat **90 min CV bike:** easy to mod	Recovery Day
WEEK 8	**4000m test swim:** 800m + 4x25m WU. 5x400m test set. 1000m CD **5k fast run:** Tempo time trial. 15 min WU. 5k fast	**75 min mod bike:** trainer: 3x20 min, 2 min RI. 11 min CD	**3000m swim:** 600, 4x75 WU. 4x100, 1x800 fast, 6x100 desc. 6x50 CD **90 min easy run:** 4 min run, 1 min walk. Repeat	**30 min swim:** 5 min easy, 20 min steady, 5 min very easy	**180 min bike:** easy to mod rolling hills, seated **15 min easy run:** transition run	**45 min swim:** open water, steady **40 min mod run:** 4 min run, 1 min walk. Repeat **60 min CV bike:** easy to mod	Recovery Day

Key: build swim = increase pace throughout workout; CD = cool-down; CV = cadence variance, varying pace throughout; m = metre; desc swim = swim in which each interval is faster than the last; env run = envelope run focussing on technique not effort; min = minute;

TRAINING PLAN

	DAY 1	DAY 2	DAY 3	DAY 4	DAY 5	DAY 6	DAY 7
WEEK 9	**2900m swim:** 400m, 8x50m WU. 2x500m, 2x250m, 5x100m. 100m CD **40 min run:** 10 min WU+CD. 20 sec fast, 40 easy	**105 min easy run:** 4 min run, 1 min walk. Repeat	**3200m mod swim:** 300, 200, 100, 12x25 4x(300 mod, 2x75 fast), 400. 100 CD **75 min mod bike:** trainer: 3x20 min, 2 min RI. 11 min CD	**30 min mod swim:** 5 min easy WU+CD. 20 min steady	**150 min bike:** 30 min easy, 120 min mod **30 min easy run:** transition run, 4 min run, 1 min walk. Repeat	**180 min bike:** easy to mod rolling hills, seated **15 min easy run:** transition run	**Recovery Day**
WEEK 10	**2800m desc swim:** 10x50m, 300m pull WU. 8x100m pull, 400m, 8x50m pull, 200m. 200m CD **50 min easy run:** 4 min run, 1 min walk. Repeat	**120 min easy run:** 4 min run, 1 min walk. Repeat	**2800m swim:** 800 WU. 4x(50 SA, 100), 3x(25 easy, 75 fast, 300 mod). 200 CD **75 min mod bike:** trainer: 3x20 min, 2 min RI. 11 min CD	**30 min swim:** 5 min easy, 20 min steady, 5 min very easy	**180 min bike:** 30 min easy, 150 min mod **30 min easy run:** transition run, 4 min run, 1 min walk. Repeat	**120 min mod bike:** flat to gently rolling course	**Recovery Day**
WEEK 11	**3100m desc swim:** 600m WU. 8x150m pull, 8x100m pull, 8x50m pull. 100m CD **50 min easy run:** 7 min run, 1 min walk. Repeat	**120 min easy run:** 4 min run, 1 min walk. Repeat	**4500m fast swim:** 300m WU+CD. 4x25m, 8x75m, 3x400m, 3x30m0, 3x200m, 5x100m **75 min mod bike:** trainer: 3x20 min, 2 min RI. 11 min CD	**30 min swim:** 5 min easy, 20 min steady, 5 min very easy	**180 min bike:** 30 min easy, 150 min mod **30 min easy run:** transition run, 4 min run, 1 min walk. Repeat	**45 min swim:** open water, steady **120 min mod bike:** flat to gently rolling course	**Recovery Day**
WEEK 12	**4000m test swim:** 800m + 4x25m WU. 5x400m test set. 1000m CD **60 min easy run:** 9 min run, 1 min walk. Repeat	**86 min mod bike:** trainer: 4x20 min, 2 min RI	**2500m swim:** 500m WU. 4x200m, 150m, 50m, 600m pull, 16x25m desc. 200m CD	**Recovery Day**	**210 min bike:** 30 min easy, 180 min mod **30 min easy run:** transition run, 4 min run, 1 min walk. Repeat	**120 min easy run:** 4 min run, 1 min walk. Repeat **45 min swim:** open water, steady **60 min CV bike:** easy to mod	**Recovery Day**
WEEK 13	**4400m swim:** 400, 300 pull, 200 WU. 4x(400, 200), 2x400. 300 CD **86 min mod bike:** trainer: 4x20 min, 2 min RI	**60 min env run:** Easy up to fast pace. Focus on technique	**2900m desc swim:** 800m WU. 3x300m, 3x200m, 5x100m. 100m CD **60 min CV bike:** easy to mod	**30 min swim:** 5 min easy, 20 min steady, 5 min very easy	**210 min bike:** 30 min easy, 180 min mod **30 min easy run:** transition run, 4 min run, 1 min walk. Repeat	**120 min easy run:** 4 min run, 1 min walk. Repeat **120 min easy bike:** Shortly after run	**Recovery Day**
WEEK 14	**2700m swim:** 10x50, 300 pull WU. 2x400, 2x300, 2x200. 100 CD **86 min mod bike:** trainer: 4x20 min, 2 min RI	**60 min env run:** Easy up to fast pace. Focus on technique	**60 min CV bike:** easy to mod **2500m desc swim:** 2x300m WU. 6x150m pull, 6x100m pull, 6x50m pull. 100m CD	**50 min swim:** 5 min easy, 40 min steady, 5 min very easy	**210 min bike:** 30 min easy, 180 min mod **15 min easy run:** transition run	**120 min easy run:** 4 min run, 1 min walk. Repeat **60 min CV bike:** easy to mod	**Recovery Day**
WEEK 15	**4000m test swim:** 800m + 4x25m WU. 5x400m test set. 1000m CD **5k fast run:** Tempo time trial. 15 min WU. 5k fast	**86 min mod bike:** trainer: 4x20 min, 2 min RI	**3400m swim:** 2x300, 200 WU. 4x300, 2x200, 1x300, 10x50. 200 CD **60 min env run:** Easy to fast pace. Focus on technique	**Recovery Day** **Race Plan:** Write out plan, starting from wake up; include schedule, nutrition, pacing	**120 min bike:** 30 min easy, 90 min mod **15 min easy run:** transition run	**3400m swim:** 3000 steady - every 100m go fast for 25m. 400 CD. **60 min CV bike:** easy to mod	**Recovery Day**
WEEK 16	**2800m swim:** 3x300 WU. 3x200, 1x1000 desc. 300 CD **45 min env run:** Easy to fast pace. Focus on technique	**49 min mod bike:** trainer: 2x20 min, 2 min RI. 5 min CD	**Recovery Day**	**2100m swim:** 10x50, 300m pull WU. 2x300m, 2x200m, 2x100m. 100 CD **40 min easy run:** 4 min run, 1 min walk. Repeat	**Recovery Day**	**Pre-race brick:** 20 min swim, 30 min bike, 15 min run; 2-3 race efforts on each, preferably on race course	**RACE DAY** Good luck!

mod = moderate; pull = use pull buoy or paddles; RI = recovery interval; S+S = stand and sit; SA = swimming with single-arm; SL = pedaling with single-leg; trainer = stationary bike; transition run = easy run immediately after bike; test swim = swim at race pace; WU = warm-up

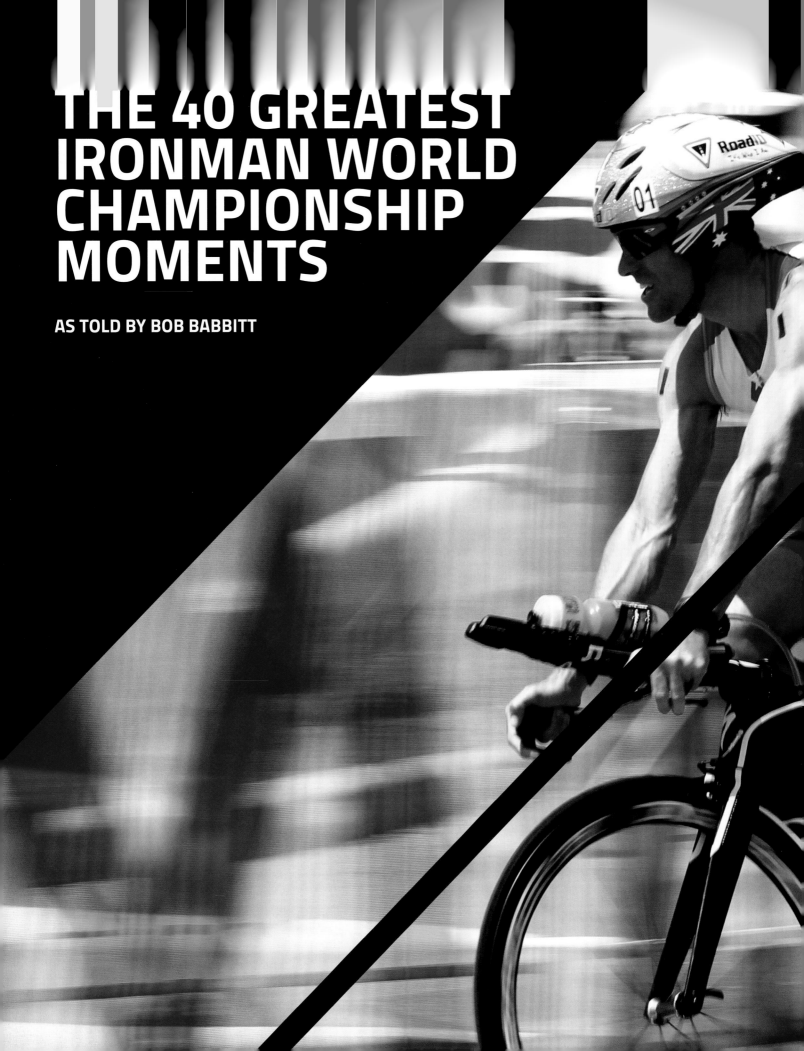

THE 40 GREATEST IRONMAN WORLD CHAMPIONSHIP MOMENTS

AS TOLD BY BOB BABBITT

I've had the good fortune of being at every IRONMAN® World Championship race in Hawai`i since 1980 when I first participated on the island of O'ahu with 107 other IRONMAN participants. Since then, I have been consistently amazed by the heroic abilities of the athletes. I am not alone. Interest in the tenacity and the breathtaking achievements of competitors has continued to grow over the years all around the world, with coverage of the IRONMAN World Championship expanding to meet the increasing demand in media outlets, as well as on ironman.com itself.

Over the first 40 years of IRONMAN's existence, fans have had the opportunity to witness some very special moments. These iconic snapshots show the best of the competitors and have taken their place in the history and fabric of the world's most important one-day endurance event. Each one demonstrates the incredible impact of the race on those who take part – it changes lives in a way that few other sporting events can do. Yes, the IRONMAN World Championship shows elite athletes accomplishing astonishing feats, but it's about so much more. It allows average people to test their spirit and their physical abilities on a day when success is often simply finishing. What each of these moments over four decades of guts and determination shows us is that anyone can have that transcendent "You are an IRONMAN" finish-line moment on Ali'i Drive. These are the moments that embody what IRONMAN stands for.

Every year, for those fortunate enough to have the opportunity to take on the lava fields of the Island of Hawai`i, lives are changed for the better. Here, in chronological order, are some of the most iconic moments in IRONMAN history.

◀ Craig Alexander, one of the great IRONMAN champions whose exploits provide the inspirational stories in this chapter.

1 # THE FIRST FINISH

▲ A group of the 1978 IRONMAN finishers showing off their original t-shirts and trophies at a reunion.

▶ Gordon Haller, the winner of the first-ever IRONMAN triathlon, in action.

There were 12 competitors who finished the first-ever IRONMAN triathlon, including co-founder John Collins. From the very beginning, the winning spirit of the high-achieving amateur was established. Gordon Haller was a taxi-cab driver, who became the pioneering IRONMAN athlete in a time of 11 hours, 46 minutes and 40 seconds. Collins himself came in at a little over 17 hours. Archie Hapai had led the field when they finished the swim, when he was followed by John Dunbar, who finished the bike with a 13-minute lead over Haller. The story of the remainder of the race day was a battle between Haller and Dunbar. Overall, Haller was the faster marathon runner, but he needed a number of rubdowns from his support crew throughout the run to combat the cramping that stopped him at various stages. He chased and caught Dunbar at the 17 and 20-mile points, but each time his breaks allowed Dunbar to stay with him. Haller was finally able to cruise away over the last five miles to book himself a place in IRONMAN history. His marathon time was 3 hours 30 minutes. Dunbar finished second, just ahead of third-placed Dave Orlowski.

THE FIRST OF MANY

1979

IRONMAN triathlon has offered both men and women an equal shot at proving themselves from its earliest days. In 1979, at the second-ever IRONMAN race, Lyn Lemaire became the first woman to get to the finish line. She was an impressive athlete by any standard. Lemaire swam in four national championships in high school and also played basketball for UCLA. She went on to be one of the best U.S. cyclists, winning the 1976 and 1977 National Time Trial Championships and was well-placed to battle her way through the IRONMAN challenge. She stormed through the cycling field to record a bike split of 6 hours 30 minutes, second only to overall champion Tom Warren. During the ride, she pulled into second place overall and, at the end of the day, her time of 12 hours 55 minutes 38 seconds put her in fifth place. Lyn Lemaire embodied something that remains true today: it doesn't matter in an IRONMAN race if an athlete is big or small, male or female, or where they come from. Anyone can make it to the finish line.

Women have also played key roles in the development, leadership and growth of the IRONMAN brand. Valerie Silk took over the young event after the 1980 race and moved it to the Big Island the following year. When prize money was introduced in 1986, Silk ensured it was divided equally between the winning men and women. This was a unique innovation in endurance sports history and the IRONMAN brand has continued to trail blaze over the years.

▼ The first female finisher: Lyn Lemaire receiving attention on the sidewalk on her way to finishing in fifth place overall.

3 TRIATHLON COMES TO TV AND MAGAZINES

IRONMAN took a huge leap forward in the public mind when US sports magazine *Sports Illustrated* showcased the second IRONMAN triathlon. The magazine ran an eight-page feature on the IRONMAN World Championship race. It focused on a San Diego-based tavern owner and IRONMAN World Champion, Tom Warren, whose passion for extreme sports caught the popular imagination when people got the chance to read about his exploits. As a result of the win and the publicity that followed the article, Warren became the first triathlete to appear on *The Tonight Show Starring Johnny Carson*. The legendary talk-show host skillfully showcased Warren's individuality, his ability to take on challenges without conforming to what anyone else was doing and the way in which he showed a spirit that wouldn't be dampened by adversity. For the huge audience watching at home, IRONMAN suddenly seemed like something that could be possible for anyone. It would be far from the last time that IRONMAN was featured on television. By the following year, IRONMAN was featured on the long-running ABC's *Wide World of Sports* and in the end would have its own primetime slot.

▼ Tom Warren bikes past the views of Mokolii Island in the background while cycling his way to victory.

CHANGING THE GAME

4

◄ John Howard racing in the Stars and Stripes of the American team during the 1976 Olympic Games.

When John Howard showed up on the starting line at the 1980 IRONMAN World Championship, it was a huge moment for the event. Howard was a Pan American Games gold medalist in cycling and a three-time Olympian. As the most-decorated athlete in the field, he was the overwhelming favorite, primarily because of his cycling prowess.

Unfortunately for John, he found out that day that the IRONMAN World Championship is way more than a bike race and, after a 1:51 swim and a 4:13 marathon, Howard left town with a fast bike ride (4:28) and a third-place finish. What did he do? He went to work, and in 1981 he swam 1:11 – 40 minutes faster than the year before – ran 3:23 – nearly an hour faster – and became the IRONMAN World Champion. In 1980, John Howard was a great cyclist. A year later, he was a great triathlete.

John Howard was the first world-class single-sport champion to embrace the triathlon challenge and he brought enhanced attention to IRONMAN and the sport of triathlon from the mainstream cycling community.

THE CRAWL

5

1982

In February 1982, two young college students changed the course of IRONMAN history. Julie Moss led deep into the marathon and for a while it looked as if she might be the champion. Then she simply ran out of gas – this was before proper race nutrition was fully understood. As she staggered towards the finish on Ali'i Drive, falling and then getting up again, Kathleen McCartney, who was in second, passed her for the win. When Moss collapsed within mere yards of the line, McCartney passed her for the win. But Moss wasn't about to give up. With the world watching on ABC's *Wide World of Sports*, Moss crawled inch-by-inch to the finish and threw her arm across that magical line. This was an electric moment for those watching on TV and Moss won the hearts of all those who witnessed this legendary finish. ABC's Jim McKay, among the most experienced sports broadcasters in history, called it the most inspiring sports moment he had ever witnessed. The IRONMAN World Championship was changed that day, from an event created for the world's top athletes to one that anyone looking for the ultimate challenge could try. And they did: 580 had entered the first of two IRONMAN races in 1982. For the second – after Moss and McCartney – the number jumped to 850. Competing became such a hot ticket that organizers instituted a qualifying system to keep the race field more manageable.

▼ Julie Moss crawls towards the finish line on hands and knees in one of the most dramatic moments in IRONMAN World Championship history.

6 / 33 SECONDS

Every second counts, even over the full distance of an IRONMAN event. Take the example of the epic struggles between Scott Tinley and Dave Scott. In February 1982, Tinley came to Kailua-Kona and beat Dave Scott in his very first encounter with him at the IRONMAN World Championship. By the end of the day's contest, Scott had come in second and Tinley was the overall winner. In the October event of the same year, they reversed roles and Scott won with Tinley taking second place. The struggle between the two athletes continued into 1983, when Dave Scott outswam Tinley by six and a half minutes and Tinley returned the favor by

out-splitting him on the bike by nearly seven minutes. During the marathon, Scott built up a lead, but towards the end of the run the wheels started to come off. The two of them were almost neck and neck but Tinley realized too late that first place was just up the road and, as he sprinted down Ali'i Drive, he could actually see Scott staggering across the finish. Dave Scott finished first in 9 hours 5 minutes 57 seconds; Scott Tinley finished 33 seconds behind him with a time of 9 hours 6 minutes 30 seconds. To this day, it is still the closest finish of the men's race in the history of the IRONMAN World Championship.

▲ Dave Scott (left) and Scott Tinley (right) thrill the crowds while crossing the finish line in the closest-ever IRONMAN World Championship finish.

7 / THE TWINS

1984

To have one IRONMAN athlete in the family is an achievement, but to have two – and identical twins at that – is something else entirely. Sylviane and Patricia Puntous came from Canada and dominated the IRONMAN World Championship in 1983 and 1984. Not only were they twins, but Sylviane's wins – she beat her sister on both occasions – marked the first by a non-USA athlete in the event's history. Yet in many ways it didn't matter so much which of them won, as the two were seen by their triathlon fans as one incredible team. They would go on to race around the world as possibly the first professional women in a sport that was truly finding itself during the early 1980s. "Hawai`i is such a special place," Patricia says. "It makes you think you can do so much once you've finished there. You're always looking for another challenge." Their Kona appearances led to years at the top of the sport and they were exhausted by the early 1990s. It wasn't until 1999 that they appeared once again on the athletics scene in Canada in a low-key form. By the end of their careers, between them they had racked up a total of seven placings in IRONMAN history – the two wins and then five second-place finishes in 1983, 1984, 1986, 1987 and 1989.

▶ The Puntous twins running in perfect unison, as they did so often throughout their incredible careers.

8 / STARTING THE TECHNOLOGY REVOLUTION

1985

▲ The aerobars that revolutionized the IRONMAN event. When Scott Tinley picked up his bike the next day he found that they had cracked immediately after the race, but fortunately they had lasted long enough to see him through to the finish.

Scott Tinley was riding an impressive-looking bike as he headed towards his second IRONMAN World Championship title. It wasn't just a flashy-looking machine but an unmistakable sign of the aero revolution to come in the sport of triathlon. Showcasing a fully aero frame, helmet and other details to enhance the efficiency of his bike position, Tinley turned the attention and focus of the industry toward developing these innovations. It was just one year later that the first triathlon bars appeared in the sport.

Bike technology had changed very little for almost 50 years and triathletes had up to now made it through the bike leg of their races on whatever they could find. In this landscape, Tinley couldn't have made a more futuristic appearance on the field than if he'd travelled in the DeLorean that was featured in that year's *Back to the Future* feature film. His speed machine's most striking feature was a set of specially built Aerosports handlebars. Even his cables were hidden in the frame to make it more aerodynamic and Tinley himself wore booties, or toe-covers, over his cycling shoes to reduce wind resistance. The technology helped him set a new course record and began the move towards the creation of what might be recognized now as a triathlon bike. Thanks to IRONMAN, it was the dawn of an experimental era for the industry that has dramatically shaped the bike industry as a whole.

9 PAULA NEWBY-FRASER WINS FOR THE FIRST TIME

1986

She is known as the "Queen of Kona," but back in 1986, the future eight-time world champion Paula Newby-Fraser was not expecting her first win. That year she thought she was going to have to be content with coming in second, as Patricia Puntous was ahead of her. It came as a total surprise when Newby-Fraser saw the finish tape being held out for her to break as she came towards the line. It turned out that Patricia had been disqualified for drafting earlier in the race. The fact that Patricia and sister Sylviane were almost impossible to tell apart had delayed the announcement of the judgment. Race officials let Patricia continue into the run because they weren't sure they'd got the right sister. That year also saw the debut of Erin Baker, but it wasn't until 1987 that Baker took the title, beating Sylviane into second place and Newby-Fraser into third. The battle for supremacy between Paula Newby-Fraser and Erin Baker had begun. Baker took the women's race to a new level in 1987; Newby-Fraser and the Puntous twins used to walk through the aid stations during the run and take little breaks, while Baker never stopped running to take a break.

Newby-Fraser says of Baker: "She became the motivating factor for me. She was the single factor that pushed me to a higher level at that time. I always felt that she was a better, more gifted athlete than I am. I always felt like I was the underdog."

▼ Savouring another victorious run up Ali'i Drive in first place in 1991; Newby-Fraser won the IRONMAN World Championship an incredible eight times.

10 SIGN OF THINGS TO COME

Having been beaten by Erin Baker in 1987, Paula Newby-Fraser was back the following year, although her arch-rival didn't take part in the event this year. The race marked the 10th anniversary of IRONMAN and Newby-Fraser had something special to help her celebrate. She had been overhauling her tactics and ran the entire marathon leg without any walking stops, giving everyone a taste of what the future held for triathlon and IRONMAN. Her hard work in fine-tuning her performance paid off as she took an incredible 34 minutes off the course record – to hit 9 hours 1 minute 1 second – and

finished eleventh overall of every single person out there, male or female competitor. Her showing that day remains one of the greatest performances in endurance sports history, in the process resetting the athletic level for women's performances. Now the 9-hour barrier was the next target for female competitors, although for Newby-Fraser there was also something further to achieve – becoming the first woman in the event's history to achieve three wins, which she duly accomplished the following year. Her extraordinary IRONMAN career was well underway.

▲ Paula Newby-Fraser had her head down, focusing hard through the lava fields on her way to an incredible course record in 1988.

11 IRON WAR

▲ The iconic Iron War. Dave Scott (left) and Mark Allen (right) were literally side by side for the majority of the day.

Throughout the 1980s, every winter the IRONMAN World Championship would air on ABC's *Wide World of Sports*. And every year from 1982 through 1989, the storyline for the men's race was exactly the same: Mark Allen, the world's best triathlete for 11 months of the year, would return to Kailua-Kona to go head-to-head with Dave Scott, the man who owned the IRONMAN title. They met for the first time in October 1982. Allen's derailleur fell off his bike as he was riding with Scott, and he had to DNF. In 1983, Scott won again and Allen took third. In 1984, Allen built an 11-minute 30-second lead on Scott by the end of the bike, fell apart in the run, and took fifth, as Scott won again. In both 1986 and 1987, Allen took second to Scott.

When Scott pulled out the night before the 1988 race, the stage was set for Allen to finally win the IRONMAN World Championship. His tires went flat twice and he took fifth. This set up 1989. It was only right: if Allen

was ever going to win the IRONMAN World Championship, it should be when he needed to knock off Dave Scott. The day was epic. Allen wore yellow and Scott wore green. They stayed together all day long until Allen got away from Scott on the last uphill on the course. When the dust had cleared, Dave Scott had broken his own course record by 18 minutes and had gone 8 hours 10 minutes 13 seconds. He ran 2 hours 41 minutes 3 seconds, the fastest marathon ever up until that day. But Mark Allen ran 2 hours 40 minutes 4 seconds, which remained the fastest marathon run at the IRONMAN World Championship until Patrick Lange finally broke the record in 2016. The legacy of this race showed the triathlon world that athletes could not just endure and "finish" an IRONMAN World Championship, but that they now had the capacity to compete and race with intensity for the full 8 hours.

12 # FATHER'S DAY

What would most fathers do if doctors told them that, as a result of oxygen deprivation to their son's brain, there was little chance of him living a normal life – and that he should be institutionalized? If they are Dick Hoyt, they ignore the experts and prove everyone wrong.

Team Hoyt began with Dick pushing son Rick in a special wheelchair at short running events, quickly moving up to the marathon. The Boston Marathon in the early years wanted nothing to do with Dick and Rick. To qualify to get into their hometown marathon, 40-year-old Dick had to run under 2:50, a time that would qualify Rick, who was in his twenties. So they went to the Marine Corps Marathon and Dick pushed Rick to an unbelievable 2:45:23, forcing Boston to let them in: now father and son are honored with a bronze statue on the course.

When it came to IRONMAN, Dick would pull Rick with a bungee attached to an inflatable boat, ride with Rick in a specially built seat on the handlebars of his bike so Dick could keep him fed and hydrated throughout, and then push Rick in a custom-made jogger during the marathon. In 1989, they completed the swim in 1:54:06, their bike ride was 8:01:30 even though the combined weight of Dick, Rick, and the bike was 376 pounds. Then Dick ran 4:30:27 for the marathon while pushing Rick, for a finishing time of 14:26:04. Together, they have completed six IRONMAN races.

▶ The bronze statue honoring the incredible father–son duo located across the road from the start line of the Boston Marathon.

▼ Team Hoyt with a new bike configuration in 2003. They returned to Kailua-Kona a number of times over the years.

13 JUST LIKE JIM

In 1985, Jim MacLaren was a 300-pound football player at Yale taking acting classes in New York City. On his way to class one day on his motorcycle, he was hit by a bus and thrown 90 feet into the air. He was declared dead on arrival but somehow survived. He was, however, severely injured, with the result that his left leg was amputated below the knee. IRONMAN, the organization recognized as a leader in the integration of physically challenged athletes in triathlon, welcomed him into the field of triathlon. They had taken great care to grow the participation of athletes from all backgrounds and encouraged the determination and extraordinary abilities of those who face their own challenges. MacLaren, on a walking leg, ran a 3:16 marathon before entering the IRONMAN World Championship and recording a time of 10:42:50 in Kailua-Kona in 1989.

Devastatingly, in June 1993, tragedy struck again, this time while MacLaren was racing in Mission Viejo, California. A van went through an intersection that had been closed for the event, hit the back of his bike and propelled him head first into a lamp post. He was now an amputee and a quadriplegic. IRONMAN remained a viable event for him. Through a group of friends, MacLaren managed to get on a special flight that October to Kona. He was fragile and weak when he emerged that year in his power chair to take center-stage at the IRONMAN Welcome Party. His IRONMAN family stood as one to welcome him back to Hawai`i and it was instrumental in his mental recovery. Everything changed for him that night – he got the glint in his eye back. The lava fields had been the site of some of his biggest achievements and, from the reaction of the crowd, he knew deep in his soul that he was valued and loved more than ever.

After Jim's second accident, the Challenged Athletes Foundation was created to help keep challenged athletes active. Since then, the charity has raised nearly $100 million and distributed more than 23,000 individual grants.

◄ The ever-courageous and always inspirational Jim MacLaren competing in the 1992 IRONMAN World Championship, the year before his second accident.

▶ Mark Allen celebrating the final moments of his IRONMAN career as he crosses the finish line in 1995.

BREAKING THE U.S. DOMINANCE
1994

The dominance of male U.S. athletes in IRONMAN racing finally came to an end in 1994 when, for the first time, it wasn't an athlete from the birthplace of the event who won the male race. This was the start of many years of winners from all over the globe and it all came about because of the success of Australia's Greg Welch. He had burst on to the scene at the 1989 IRONMAN World Championship when he finished a distant third behind Mark Allen and Dave Scott. Welch won the ITU World Championship at Disney World the following year, establishing him as one of the best in triathlon. But despite his brilliance, he still had a ways to go. He finished fifth at Kona in 1990, second in 1991 and then sixth in 1992. He was one of the favorites leading into the 1993 IRONMAN World Championship until injury prevented him from taking part. In 1994, Jürgen Zäck, one of the premier cyclists in the sport, took off after the turnaround in Hawi. In the past, Greg Welch might have chased, but not this time. "I thought about what I learned from watching last year," he said. "Jürgen likes to do this thing off the front. 'I'm not going to be suckered into that,' I said to myself. 'I want to have a good run.'" Deep into the marathon, Greg Welch was leading the way with 40-year-old IRONMAN legend Dave Scott bearing down on him. His lead expanded as he came out of the Natural Energy Lab and headed back to downtown Kailua-Kona. He leaped across the line with the Australian flag in tow. Welch's win set the stage for the next two decades of international winners from around the globe.

▲ His face paints the perfect picture as Greg Welch leaps across the line to become the first non-U.S. male athlete to win the IRONMAN World Championship.

15

GOING OUT ON TOP
1995

Mark Allen, after finally defeating Dave Scott in their classic Iron War showdown in 1989, then managed four straight wins. He took 1994 off and the plan was to come back in 1995 and, hopefully, win the IRONMAN World Championship one last time. But at the age of 37, Allen wasn't sure if his body could manage one last win. Especially when Thomas Hellriegel flew by him on the bike and took a 13:31 lead into the marathon.

Allen knew that in order to have a chance, he'd have to make up 30 seconds every mile. There is a huge difference between running a 2:42 marathon when in the lead and having to run a 2:42 to win the race. "I was having discussions with myself," remembers Allen. "This is too tough. I can't make up that much ground. It's not my day. I've won this race five times, do I really need to win it again?" Eventually, he silenced that voice and instead focused on each step, each mile. Hellriegel was running well, putting together a 2:58:05 marathon, which on most days would have won him the title.

But this wasn't most days. Mark Allen ended up tying Dave Scott with six IRONMAN World Championship titles by posting a 2:42:09 marathon, catching Hellriegel in the closing miles and winning the most important event in his sport. The oldest winner at the time, he retired on top of his game.

16 HEART BEATS GEAR ANY DAY

IRONMAN races are about pushing to the absolute limit to discover one's best. They test body, mind, and spirit – all things that can't be bought at a price. This was demonstrated in 1996, when Dr. Cory Foulk set himself a $20 limit for purchasing gear for the race. Dr. Foulk turned up at the event on his 61-pound Schwinn Typhoon (about three times what many of today's athletes' bikes weigh), which he had bought for $15. When he got to the transition area, he was told he couldn't bring a bike with a kickstand; he then had to put it back on when the officials realized his tires were too thick to fit the bike rack! Foulk came out of the swim, put on his Hawaiian shirt, and rode 112 miles barefoot on his cruiser bike with only one gear. This intrepid competitor proved his point in the end, making all the cut off times. He rode the bike in 8 hours 50 minutes 21 seconds and showed that it's the athlete that matters at IRONMAN races, not what that athlete spends on equipment.

Similarly, In 2010, Tim Winestorfer rode a wooden bike during the IRONMAN World Championship (he called it "Mother Nature's carbon fiber"). The bike was made from padauk and black walnut. Winestorfer finished the bike course with a time of 5:30:33 (and overall course time of 11:57:12) and showed once again that it is the athlete that matters. The bike he rode was manufactured by Southeast Portland-based Renovo Hardwood Bicycles. Tim went back to Kona in 2013, and although he still owns his wooden bike decided not to race in it that year.

▲▲ Not your avarage IRONMAN outfit! But Foulk proved that even on a $15 bike with a basket and a kickstand, if an athlete's heart and determination is great enough, they can still be an IRONMAN finisher.

▲ Tim Winestorfer's Mother Nature's carbon-fiber (wooden) bike he rode in 2010 with a bike course time of 5:30:33

17 COOL HAND LUC

Conventional wisdom would suggest that an athlete has to rack up a great deal of experience to be an IRONMAN champion. But part of what makes the challenge so unique is that the individual athlete can always achieve something surprising – often for themselves and their watching family and supporters, but occasionally something that takes the whole world by surprise. This was certainly true of Luc Van Lierde, who had never run a marathon – much less entered an IRONMAN event – before he found himself on the starting line in Kailua-Kona in 1996. The Belgian hopeful was not intimidated by the spotlight. Despite getting a drafting infraction during the bike ride and having to serve three minutes in the penalty box after the ride, Van Lierde ran 2 hours 41 minutes 48 seconds in the marathon to take the title and, in the process, broke Mark Allen's course record by five minutes – going 8 hours 4 minutes 8 seconds. It was an unmatched performance and a day that would go down in the IRONMAN World Championship history books. His record would stand for 15 years until Craig Alexander finally broke it in 2011. Van Lierde's unorthodox approach might not be advisable for every newcomer, but he dug out something special in a race where every athlete brings their own magic.

▶ Luc Van Lierde (left) and Thomas Hellriegel (right) were arm in arm as they waved to the crowd at the end of the 1996 race. Hellriegel finished just two minutes behind the record-breaking Belgian.

18 THIRD TIME'S THE CHARM

▲ Worth the wait: Hellriegel relishes his chance to finally break the tape after winning the 1997 IRONMAN World Championship.

Thomas Hellriegel was the most consistent men's performer in Kailua-Kona towards the end of the 1990s and into the 2000s, never finishing out of the top ten. Yet winning an IRONMAN World Championship eluded him for some time. But just as athletes don't let the rigors of race day defeat them, he had to play the long game to reach his prize. He endured a crazy lifestyle that saw him travelling from training camp to training camp through the German winter – preparations for one season included three-week stints on two Canary Islands, Lanzarote and Tenerife, and one in Mallorca. In the 1995 IRONMAN World Championship race, he came out of the ocean three and a half minutes down to five-time IRONMAN World Champion Mark Allen. Next, he out-split Allen on the bike 4 hours 29 minutes 37 seconds to 4 hours 46 minutes 35 seconds. It meant that Hellriegel had a lead going into the marathon of over 13 minutes. He followed that up with a 2-hour 58-minute 5-second marathon, which should have sealed the deal. But Allen caught Hellriegel at about mile 22, and, in his final race, at the age of 37, won his sixth title, with Hellriegel in second. In 1996 Hellriegel again put together a great race, but fell foul of the unknown Luc Van Lierde to come in second, again. But as is so often the case in endurance sport, persistence, patience and practice paid off. In 1997, with a slower time than he posted in both 1995 and 1996, Hellriegel became the first German to win the IRONMAN World Championship title and, ironically, with Jürgen Zäck in second and Lothar Leder in third, he led a German 1-2-3 sweep.

19 RISING TO THE CHALLENGE 1997

In 1994, Dr. Jon Franks became the first paralyzed athlete to attempt the IRONMAN World Championship using a hand cycle and a racing chair. He missed the bike cut-off time in his one and only attempt at Kona. In 1995, paraplegic John Maclean from Australia attempted to do the same, and he too missed the bike cut-off time. He was so tired that it took him three attempts to put an Australian flag on the back of his wheelchair. In 1996, despite a 1-hour 5-minute swim time, Maclean got a flat tire on the bike course and missed the cut-off time by just 15 minutes. However, he was asked to do the marathon in his racing chair anyway to see if a paralyzed athlete could indeed go under the 17-hour mark. He did.

Maclean didn't quit and returned in 1997, when he easily made all of the cut-off times. He finished in 12 hours 21 minutes and became the first wheelchair athlete to cross the finish line at the IRONMAN World Championship. Another athlete competing that year, Clarinda Brueck had been born without the lower portion of her left arm. She said of IRONMAN, "I want physically challenged children to feel what I felt when I first competed in a triathlon. For the first time in my life, I felt I was competing with, and even excelling above, able-bodied individuals. That's an empowering, life-changing experience." Formal divisions for both hand-cycle athletes, like Dr. Jon Franks and John Maclean, and physically challenged athletes, like Clarinda Brueck, were established in 1997. Such was the immediate interest that qualifying races were established for hand-cycle athletes to qualify for the World Championship.

▶ Jim Maclean broke new ground with his hand cycle performance in 1997, empowering the next generation of physically challenged athletes.

20 FINISHING IS WINNING

Some 15 years after Julie Moss's epic crawl to the finish had helped put IRONMAN and the sport of triathlon on the map, Wendy Ingraham and Sian Welch were entering the last mile of the marathon. Since Heather Fuhr had already won and Lori Bowden had taken second place, Ingraham and Welch were both hoping to seize the final spot on the podium.

Welch passed a cramping Ingraham at the top of Palani Road, and seemed to be in the driver's seat. But as she headed down Ali'i Drive towards the finish, her legs started to wobble and she collapsed to the pavement just as Fernanda Keller from Brazil flew by her to take that coveted final podium position from her.

So now the battle was for fourth and fifth. As she struggled to get to her feet, Welch saw Ingraham striding towards her in what looked to be a new both-legs-are-totally-cramping style of race walking. Welch used the fencing and the banners to try and get to her feet, but her legs wouldn't hold her and she went back to the ground, this time bumping into Ingraham who joined her on the finish line carpet.

After a few futile attempts to get to her feet, Ingraham decided to do her best Julie Moss imitation and actually crawl the last few yards to the finish. "I saw Wendy start to crawl," remembers Welch, "and I thought that looked like a good idea."

Ingraham ended up taking fourth place by ten seconds over Welch but, as with Julie Moss 15 years earlier, the final placing was way less important than reinforcing the credo Moss had established a decade and a half earlier: when it comes to IRONMAN, finishing *is* winning.

▲ The living embodiment of a never-say-die attitude: Ingraham and Welch edge their way painfully across the finish line as the crowd wills them over.

21 SUB 3

▲ Peter Reid shouts encouragement to his wife Lori Bowden as she runs her way into the record books with the first sub 3-hour marathon time.

Paula Newby-Fraser had come close to beating the 9-hour barrier on a number of occasions and in 1992 her determination paid off. She broke her own course record by nearly five minutes, becoming the first woman ever to eclipse the mark at the IRONMAN World Championship with a historic 8 hours 55 minutes 28 seconds. That amazing performance still left goals to aim for, particularly for a woman to record the first sub 3-hour marathon at Kona. Despite the great running credentials of many athletes in previous years – including Heather Fuhr, who had come to triathlon having first been a competitive track runner in her high school and university days – the 3-hour barrier remained elusive. It was Lori Bowden who finally cracked it. After two podium finishes in previous years, Bowden claimed her debut title at the 1999 IRONMAN World Championship with the first-ever sub-3-hour marathon for a woman. She had twice come in second, but this time her 2-hour 59-minute time blasted the field into submission with her performance taking five minutes off Fuhr's 1998 run record. Bowden set the stage for the ensuing decades of great running performances to come from likes of three-time IRONMAN World Champion Mirinda Carfrae, the four-time IRONMAN World Champion and IRONMAN Hall of Fame inductee Chrissie Wellington, and Daniela Ryf, who won three consecutive IRONMAN World Championships between 2015–17.

22 THANK YOU

From 1998 to 2000, former Navy SEAL Carlos Moleda and motocross legend David Bailey went head-to-head at Kona in the handcycle division. They came from very different backgrounds: Moleda was paralyzed following a gunshot wound he recieved during a mission in Panama; Bailey was a legend in the sport of motocross and at the top of his game when he was paralyzed during a training session.

For the first two years of their competiton, Moleda took the victory. Leading into the 2000 IRONMAN World Championship, Bailey was fitter than he had ever been and the two were on a collision course for a great race.

Moleda passed Bailey going up Palani, early in the handcycle ride. Bailey caught him on the way back to town, but with six miles to go he got a flat tire and Moleda pulled away again.

However, rather than take the easy victory, Moleda pulled over to wait for his rival to change his tire and get back on the road. This time, finally, it was Bailey's turn. He got ahead of Moleda and took the win.

Rather than rush off to celebrate with his family and friends, Bailey waited for Moleda to come across the line as well. The two embraced and Bailey said, "Thank you for pushing me to a level I never would have reached on my own."

The three-year battle between the two athletes had been special, partly because the competition and athleticism on show was so intense that any thought of the word "disability" simply disappeared. But also because, come race day, there were two athletes on show who wanted nothing more than to beat each other, but had so much respect for each other that it had to be done the right way.

23 "GO USA! GO USA!"

◄ David Bailey is a picture of power while in full flow at the IRONMAN World Championship.

▲ One of the more emotional finish line moments in IRONMAN's history as Tim DeBoom holds the U.S. flag aloft.

◄ Carlos Moleda speeding downhill on his way to his second win at the IRONMAN World Championship in 1999.

The first international sporting event after the tragedy of 9/11 was inevitably a special and charged one and there was no doubt that the 2001 IRONMAN World Championship felt different. The athletes weren't even sure that it would take place that year and most were having a difficult time getting back to things that suddenly seemed so trivial: swimming, biking and running.

But when October rolled around the athletes were in position and the race went ahead. America's Tim DeBoom had lost the year before to his former training partner, Canadian Peter Reid, by a small amount. "I remember thinking at the finish," recalls DeBoom, "I lost the IRONMAN World Championship by two lousy minutes. I

knew that every time I went out for a ride, run or swim during the next 12 months, that two minutes would both haunt me and push me. Two minutes? You've got to be kidding!"

DeBoom was a man on a mission. He ran through the final miles of the marathon in first place – fittingly, given the horrors that New York had endured just weeks earlier – to become the first American to win the IRONMAN World Championship since Mark Allen in 1995. He said, "The fans weren't cheering, 'Go Tim!' They were cheering, 'Go USA! Go USA!' It gave me goose bumps." At the time of writing in 2018, he remains the last U.S. man to have won the IRONMAN World Championship in Kailua-Kona, Hawai`i.

24

FINISH WHAT YOU START

The year was 2004. Christian Sadowski had entered the race through registering for and winning the drawing spot that year, and was having a good day until about mile 105 of the bike ride. That's when a motorcycle hit him and his bike was destroyed; his front wheel was mangled and the frame was cracked.

"My first thought was that my wife was going to kill me. There's no way I can explain this to her, and the bike is only 10 months old!" he later recalled. "I had two options, but quitting the race was not going to be one of them."

He picked up his shattered bike, tossed it over his shoulder, took off his bike shoes and walked the last seven miles off the bike course to T2 in his socks. It took him two and a half hours, and he barely made the bike cut-off time, ultimately finishing the ride/walk in 8:28. Of course, he then had to worry about the marathon!

His time at the finish was 16:09, but his message was much more important than the numbers on a clock. Participating in an IRONMAN race is about dealing with whatever the day might dish out, digging deep inside yourself and finishing what you start, no matter what. No one exemplifies that better than Christian Sadowski.

◀ Christian Sadowski shows that the bike can ride him as well as he can ride it.

25

A WINNING SMILE

Nina Kraft became the only person in IRONMAN World Championship history to win the race, test positive for drugs and have her title taken away. The consequences of her drug use were felt not only by her, but also by 2004's second-placed competitor, four-time champion, Natascha Badmann, an unbelievable 17 minutes back.

Kraft's behavior had been strange that week. At the pre-race press conference, she was bundled up like a mummy and shivering. It seemed like she might have the flu. When she crossed the line that day with her huge win, there seemed to be no joy surrounding her victory. Her head was down and she never smiled.

She admitted that she felt so much pressure to win that she resorted to EPO, or erythropoietin, then the latest performance-enhancing drug to hit athletics. Besides leaving a black mark on the sport and Kraft ruining her own career, there was Natascha Badmann who, despite now being a five-time champion, certainly didn't feel like one. She didn't get to break the tape, wear the traditional wreath or speak at the awards ceremony. To make up for it, IRONMAN sent her trophy to Bob Babbitt in San Diego along with a winner's wreath and the finishing tape. Then, on stage at an annual triathlon awards event in February, Badmann's Hawai`i victory was re-created in front of an audience of 500 applauding her with a standing ovation. The woman whose smile and infectious joy always lit up the island finally had her moment in the sun, and Badmann went on to become a six-time IRONMAN World Champion.

26 UNFINISHED BUSINESS

◄ An image of pure joy as Sarah Reinertsen crosses the finish line in 2005, laying to rest her demons from the year before.

When Sarah Reinertsen first came to the IRONMAN World Championship in 2004, her goal was to become the first female above-knee amputee to finish the event. Reinertsen missed the cut-off time on the bike that day by 15 minutes.

As a young girl who had been dissuaded from the sport by her soccer coach, overcoming the odds was something Reinertsen had been doing her whole life. At 13, she became the fastest female above-the-knee amputee in history over 100m.

Stronger and more determined than ever, she returned to the IRONMAN World Championship race the following year with unfinished business. Ironically, on the 15th of the month, in 2005, her time was 15:05, making Reinertsen the first single above-knee amputee woman to finish the race in Kailua-Kona. Just as importantly, thousands of other people who watched her story play out on NBC in both 2004 and 2005 were moved by Reinertsen to overcome their own personal challenges in the years to come.

27 THE BLAZEMAN

2005

It all started in January 2005 when Jon Blais, known as Blazeman, was at a party and realized he was having problems holding on to his beer. In February, he crashed hard on his mountain bike and had to have 15 staples in his head. "I never would have had such a stupid accident if I hadn't started to lose control of my hands," he said.

Blais went online and stayed up all night trying to figure out what was wrong with him. He realized that he may have amyotrophic lateral sclerosis (ALS), also known as motor neuron disease (MND) and Lou Gehrig's disease. When he was officially diagnosed that May at the age of 33, he was told that there was no treatment and no cure and that he had two to five years to live. As he treaded water in Kailua Bay for the 2005 IRONMAN World Championship, he had no idea if he could even finish the race because his body had deteriorated so rapidly.

He completed the swim in 1:50 rather than the 1:05 he would have swam before the onset of the disease. On race day he was forced to swim with only one arm. On the bike, he couldn't get out of the saddle and his calves and quads were seizing up throughout the ride. He made the bike cut-off time and headed out on the marathon to complete the race and become the first and only person with ALS to even attempt the toughest day in sport.

When "the Voice of IRONMAN", Mike Reilly, asked Blazeman before the race what his plans were for the finish line – maybe a Greg Welch-style leap or a push-up, or ten – he responded by saying that he didn't know if he'd be able to finish, but that Reilly might need to log roll his sorry butt across the line. A tribute to its creator, the "Blazeman Roll" has become a common site at the IRONMAN finish line to honor Jon and all others who suffer from ALS.

Jon Blais passed away at the age of 35 on May 27, 2007, but the awareness he created that day – and the charity he created to help find a cure for ALS – will live on forever. "You can choose to be pissed off or pissed on," he said in an interview after the race. Blazeman, as always, chose the former.

▼ The original Blazeman Roll, which has since been performed countless times by IRONMAN finishers.

28 NEVER SAY NEVER

Michellie Jones has long been regarded as one of the most diverse triathletes in the history of the sport. But for many years there was one title that eluded her – IRONMAN World Champion – and by her own personal choice. After winning two ITU World Championships, the Xterra World Championship and winning the silver medal at the Sydney Olympic Games in 2000, the year in which the triathlon debuted as an Olympic sport, she consistently publicly declared that an IRONMAN race was something she would "never" do. However, after being left off the Australian team for the Athens Olympics in 2004, she finally decided to try her hand at longer distances. After a second-place finish in the 2005 IRONMAN World Championship behind Natascha Badmann, she returned in 2006 to add an IRONMAN World Championship title to her incredible résumé, becoming the first Australian woman to win the event. Michellie remains the most winning triathlete in the history of the sport, continuing her amazing career with a gold medal in the 2016 Rio Olympic Games as a guide for sight-impaired athlete Katie Kelly in the Paralympics. She has also been inducted into the Australia Sports Hall of Fame, ITU Hall of Fame, and the Triathlon Australia Hall of Fame.

◀ Michellie Jones biking her way to the transition during the 2006 IRONMAN World Championship.

29 THE MIRACLE

2007

In October 2005, single above-knee amputee Sarah Reinertsen finished the IRONMAN World Championship for the first time. Among those watching her achievement was Scott Rigsby. He had more cause to follow her performance than most. When he had been only 18 years old, he had been involved in a terrible motor vehicle accident – one in which he was dragged under a trailer for 300 feet. One of his legs had to be amputated right away. The other would come off a decade later after 26 operations. "I could throw a pity party," he said, "but no one would show up." He had endured several difficult and frustrating years when he saw what could be done in an IRONMAN race. His mission became clear. If a single above-knee amputee could finish Kona, could a double below-knee amputee – built like a linebacker – also tackle the toughest day in sport? In 2007, Scott Rigsby proved they could. He became the first, going 16 hours 42 minutes 46 seconds. The IRONMAN Foundation later partnered with The Scott Rigsby Foundation, which provides assistance for those with loss of limb or mobility to live an active and healthy lifestyle.

30 SPORTSMANSHIP

2008

▲▲ Scott Rigsby closing in on the finish line during the 2007 IRONMAN World Championship.

▲ Unlike her 2008 IRONMAN World Championship experience, Chrissie Wellington had no issues with her bike on the way to victory in the 2008 IRONMAN Germany.

Chrissie Wellington was in the lead during the bike race of the 2008 IRONMAN World Championship when she had a flat tire. It was a nuisance, but she was – of course – prepared. Instead of a bulky hand pump to inflate her spare, she used smaller and lighter CO_2 cartridges, which could also do the job much faster than a manual inflator. The potential drawback was that, if they should fail for any reason, then the air would be gone and the rider out of options. This was what happened to Wellington and it began to seem as if this might even be the end of her attempt at finishing, much less retaining the title she had won the previous year. She was left at the side of the road waiting for mechanical support, all the while the precious minutes ticking away. But then the incredible happened – Australian competitor Rebekah Keat gave Wellington one of her own cartridges in a remarkably selfless and sporting act that encapsulated the great spirit of IRONMAN. Yet there was still a great challenge to overcome – somehow, Wellington had to make up all that lost time. She did exactly that, even going on to finish almost a quarter of an hour ahead of the nearest challenger, in a time of 9 hours 6 minutes and 23 seconds. She followed that with a win the next year and one more in 2011.

31 THE HANDSHAKE

When Chris McCormack, or "Macca," came to Kailua-Kona, Hawai`i, for the first time in 2002, he thought he'd win the race. In a pre-race interview, he said his goal was to win the race SIX times. Fans and followers of the sport suggested he try to win it once, first. McCormack found out the hard way that it would require more dedication than perhaps he thought he'd need. He had to show he had the competitiveness in him to take the title.

In 2002, he dropped out. In 2003, he walked the marathon. In 2004, he dropped out again. In 2005, he finished sixth, he was second in 2006 by 71 seconds and, then, in 2007, on his sixth try, he finally won the biggest prize in the sport. After dropping out in 2008 and taking fourth in 2009, people thought McCormack just might be done. In 2010, at the age of 37, he arrived in Kailua-Kona lean and hungry for the first time since 2007. He pushed the pace on the bike to get away from two-time IRONMAN World Champion Craig Alexander and took the lead in the marathon. But then Germany's Andreas Raelert ran through the field and caught McCormack at about mile 22. They ran side-by-side for three miles, shared sponges and did their best to re-create the classic Mark Allen vs. Dave Scott battle of the 1989 IRONMAN World Championship. "It's like the Iron War," said Macca to Raelert as they shook hands and moved ever closer to the finish line.

Macca and Raelert crested the climb together, took a right on Palani, and started down the hill. Macca, who was fighting cramps, dug deep, and when Raelert slowed down to grab fluid at an aid station, he surged away from him. Andreas may have looked the fresher runner as they ran side-by-side, but the truth was he had simply burned too many matches closing the gap to Macca and now had absolutely nothing left.

After over eight hours of racing, the gap at the end was only 1:40, 8:10:37 to 8:12:17. Macca had proven the doubters wrong.

▼ The Handshake: even in the extreme heat of competition, Raelert and McCormack show the true IRONMAN spirit.

32 OVERCOMING THE ODDS

It was the toughest call she'd ever had to make. Three-time defending IRONMAN World Champion Chrissie Wellington was forced to drop out with a viral infection the morning of the 2010 race. Mirinda Carfrae went on to win her first IRONMAN World Championship title.

When Wellington crashed two weeks before the 2011 IRONMAN World Championship and ended up with contusions on her hip and shoulder as well as extensive road rash from her thigh to her lower leg, she and her coach Dave Scott weren't sure if she could even get to the starting line. Before the crash, Wellington knew she was in the best shape of her life heading into the 2011 race where she hoped to reclaim her title. The last thing she wanted to do was not start the world's most important triathlon for the second year in a row.

To compound the issue, doctors thought she might also have a torn pectoral muscle. A few days before the race, she had to have her wounds scrubbed out to avoid infection. While her training pointed towards a 53- or 54-minute swim, she came out of the water with a big smile on her face in 1:01. This would be her thirteenth full distance race and she was undefeated. But this time she was not only

injured, she was going up against a woman who was the defending champion and was considered the best pure runner in the sport.

Wellington's margin of victory in 2007 had been about five minutes. In 2008, it was 15 minutes and, in 2009, it had ballooned to nearly 20 minutes. This was a woman who was used to dominating everywhere she raced and had never been challenged. This day would be very different, yet her victory transcended all expectations. Off the bike, she was 22 minutes behind the leader, Julie Dibens, and 10 minutes back from Rachel Joyce and Leanda Cave. Her time at the end was 8:55 and her margin of victory on Mirinda Carfrae was a mere 2:49, her closest ever at Kona.

"Those were definitely my proudest racing hours," Chrissie would say afterwards. "I was the last pro out of the water and came off the bike in sixth. I had to fight tooth and nail and I had never had to do that before. The fight is what I love, the fight is what I crave and the fight is what I got. Internally and externally I crossed that finish line physically and emotionally annihilated. I knew then that I was complete as an athlete." It turned out to be Chrissie Wellington's last race.

▶ The look of joy on her face shows that the pain was worth it. Chrissie Wellington had to put in one of the finest performances ever seen at Kona to win in 2011.

◀ Chrissie Wellington is helped to her feet after performing the Blazeman Roll in honor of her friend Jon Blais.

33 CHANGE IS GOOD

2011

▲ Craig Alexander races his way through the "Hot Corner" at the intersection of Kuakini Highway and Palani Road in 2011.

Craig Alexander had immediate success on the Kona coast. He came in second in his first attempt in 2007 and then in both 2008 and 2009 won the IRONMAN World Championship. His game plan was simple: stay within striking distance during the ride and then use his great running skills to win. But going into the 2010 race, fellow Aussie and 2007 champion Chris McCormack came up with a plan of his own.

"Craig is a front-of-the-pack swimmer," he insisted. "He is also the best runner in the heat in the sport. His one weakness is on the bike in the crosswinds out by Hawi. If everyone in the lead group works together to push the pace during that tough out and back section between Kawaihae, Hawi and then back to Kawaihae, we might be able to put some time on him. If we don't, he's going to win his third title in a row." McCormack's plan worked to perfection and Alexander was too far back off the bike to catch McCormack and came in fourth, a little over six minutes back.

A champion like Craig Alexander, however, can adapt and change the game plan. In 2011, for the first time, he wore an aero helmet and this time it was he who dictated the pace on the bike. His bike split in 2010 had been 4 hours 39 minutes 35 seconds. In 2011 it was 4 hours 24 minutes 5 seconds, more than 15 minutes faster than the year before. He had run an amazing 2 hours 41 minutes 59 seconds in 2010 and, despite going so much faster on the bike in 2011, he only lost a few minutes off his marathon time to run 2 hours 44 minutes 3 seconds.

That year Alexander became the first person to win both the IRONMAN 70.3® World Championship and IRONMAN World Championship races in the same year. He went 8 hours 3 minutes 56 seconds to break Luc Van Lierde's course record from 1996 by 12 seconds. At the same time he joined an elite club by taking his third IRONMAN World Championship title.

34 IT CAN HAPPEN

2013

Hines Ward had a successful career as a NFL wide receiver, playing 14 seasons of American football for the Pittsburgh Steelers. He was a two-time Super Bowl Champion and was voted Super Bowl XL Most Valuable Player. As illustrious as his résumé is, it is also true that there is a very different physical requirement placed on participants who want to be involved in an IRONMAN triathlon. Ward was a superstar on the field, but he had never run more than a mile in his life. He achieved his goals in football, a game all about power and fast-twitch speed. Taking on endurance was a great leveller, as he was suddenly at the same standard as many of the amateur enthusiasts on the field, but he knew what he had to do. There was a reason behind it all for him. He undertook the challenge of completing an IRONMAN race, he said, to show everyone who was "wanting to do it and questioning if they can" that he was proof that it can happen if you are willing to try. He completed the race in 13:08:15 and as a lasting reminder he got a KONA 2013 M-Dot® tattoo.

▲ The muscular Hines Ward prepares to conquer his first-ever triathlon on his road to qualify for the IRONMAN World Championship.

35

YOU NOW HAVE A PLATFORM . . . USE IT!

2013

Minda Dentler became the first woman in a hand cycle and racing chair to finish the IRONMAN World Championship on her second attempt in 2013. She has gone on to become an advocate against polio, the condition that affected her from an early age. But it took IRONMAN and its tight-knit family for her to find her focus.

Born in Bombay, now Mumbai, India, Dentler was not immunized against polio and the illness left her paralyzed from the hips down. After being placed in an orphanage, Dentler was adopted by a family from Spokane, Washington, when she was three years old and has spent her life with her legs in braces using crutches to get around. She had never been involved in sports growing up. "I tried to hide my chicken legs under pants," she remembers. "My dad and I would watch sports on TV every weekend, but I never thought that I could be an athlete."

After moving to New York City and at the age of 26, she watched the New York City Triathlon and was so inspired that she signed up and completed first the marathon and then the New York City Triathlon. After meeting top para-triathlete Jason Fowler, she signed up for an IRONMAN 70.3 event and that led to her racing the 2012 IRONMAN World Championship. She missed the bike cut-off time in her first attempt at Kona. In 2013, she returned and on this occasion made the bike by three minutes, recording an overall time of 14 hours 39 minutes 10 seconds. When she was at the IRONMAN awards ceremony the next evening, four-time IRONMAN World Champion Chrissie Wellington approached her. "Chrissie told me that I now had a platform and it was important to make use of it," she remembers. "Chrissie's comment had a huge effect on me and it changed my life." It also changed the lives of many others. With her victory, Minda Dentler was nominated for an ESPY award, and is now an advocate and ambassador for ending polio around the world.

◀ A truly inspirational moment as Minda Dentler pushes her way across the finish line, earning her place among the champions fighting to make the world a better place.

36 # DON'T GIVE IN TO THAT VOICE

2014

Daniela Ryf of Switzerland had just won the IRONMAN 70.3 World Championship title the month before the 2014 IRONMAN World Championship race. Already an Olympian, she had a natural talent to go long. After a great swim and bike, Ryf was off on the marathon in first place with Mary Beth Ellis, Jodie Swallow, Caroline Steffen and Rachel Joyce giving chase.

Australian Mirinda Carfrae, the defending champion with two IRONMAN World Championship wins to her credit, was 14:30 behind as she exited transition. That's a tough spot to be in as the defending champion, and a lot of ground to make up. It's fair to say at that moment her air-conditioned apartment might have seemed the better option. "If you give in to that voice," Carfrae said, "and quit and go home, how much pain is that going to put you in, knowing that you gave up, knowing that you gave in and knowing that you're soft? That's going to be much more pain than going through the pain of finishing the race."

Mirinda Carfrae did not quit and she gave it her all — breaking her own run course record and going 2:50:26, passing Ryf for the win with about four miles to go. "I'm over the moon," she admitted afterwards. Why? She'd not only won her third title, but had the third fastest marathon of the day overall, breaking her own run course record and overcoming one of the biggest deficits in IRONMAN World Championship history. She went 9:00:55, edging out Ryf by a mere 2:02.

▶ Mirinda Carfrae had to keep her head and not panic when chasing down Daniela Ryf in 2014, as she did while running up Palani Road.

37 THE FASTEST EVER

The first time Daniela Ryf of Switzerland came to the Island of Hawai`i was in 2014 and she knew little of the island or the race. While most of the top professionals were in town two or three weeks before the race, Ryf arrived a few days beforehand and, during a race week interview, she wondered if the road she was close to – Ali'i Drive – was actually part of the race course. She was assured that it was.

She had just won the 2014 IRONMAN 70.3 World Championship title, so there was a lot of expectation around the young woman from Switzerland. It had only been a few months before race day that her coach had suggested she give the full-distance IRONMAN race a try. She had been planning on doing the Olympic distance race at IRONMAN Switzerland, and thought the idea of switching to the full-distance IRONMAN race was downright crazy. But race it she did, and she won both the

Olympic distance race and the full-distance, which qualified her to race in the IRONMAN World Championship.

During that first race in Kailua-Kona, she led the field for most of the day before Mirinda Carfrae came storming by during the latter miles of the marathon to win her third IRONMAN World Championship title. Then in 2015, Ryf won for the first time, but Carfrae was injured in a bike crash a few days before the race and forced to drop out of the race during the bike ride; people wondered what might have happened if Mirinda Carfrae had been healthy.

Ryf obviously wanted to make sure that in 2016 there was no question of who was the best female triathlete on the course, and she put together a convincing argument. She swam 52:50, rode 4:52:26 and ran 2:56:51, and her 8:46:46 shattered the existing world record: Mirinda Carfrae took second that day and was nearly 24 minutes back in 9:10:30.

▲ Daniela Ryf spreads the Swiss flag wide with pride after becoming the fastest-ever women to complete the IRONMAN World Championship.

38 MORE THAN A RACE, A VEHICLE FOR CHANGE

2016

▲ Someone who has had to overcome more hurdles than most, Shirin Gerami thoroughly enjoyed her celebrations after finishing the 2016 IRONMAN World Championship.

Shirin Gerami came from Iran powered by a passion and drive to prove that being an athlete and accomplishing a goal should never be hindered by where an athlete is from or what they wear. She dedicated two years to creating the approved clothing and securing the necessary permissions from Iran's sports ministry for her to take to the start line at the 2016 IRONMAN World Championship race and still conform to Islamic dress codes for women. Representing her country, she became the first woman to complete the race wearing a hijab – head (though not face) covering – and the traditional Islamic clothing which covers the entire body. Considering the drag that the approved outfit had on her speed, her time of 13 hours and 11 minutes was all the more impressive. The image of Gerami coming down the finish line was one that has inspired cultural change in her country, prompting the Islamic government to support the development of women in triathlon.

39 | **2017**

THE MARK OF A CHAMPION

During the 2016 IRONMAN World Championship race, Patrick Lange from Germany had a penalty during the bike leg and finished the ride in twenty-third place. But it was obvious from the start of the marathon that Lange was a man on a mission and the heat of the lava fields wasn't going to slow him down in the least. He ran 2:39:45, broke Mark Allen's run-course record, and rounded out an all-German podium behind Jan Frodeno and Sebastian Kienle.

In 2017, Lange came off the bike around 10 minutes down to Canada's Lionel Sanders and once again ran his way through the field like a hot knife through butter. There was one difference this time around. In order to win his first IRONMAN World Championship title by a mere 2:27, Patrick Lange had to put together a 2:39:59 marathon in order to catch Sanders in the last two miles and, in the process, break three-time champion Craig Alexander's 2011 IRONMAN World Championship course record.

Many athletes through the years have come off the bike 10 minutes off the pace and run their way into the top ten. But to get off the bike over 10 minutes back to Lionel Sanders, an athlete who was on his way to running a solid 2:51 marathon, and to go 8:01:40 and break the course record to win the race?

That is the mark of a true champion.

▼ Patrick Lange lets out a roar of joy after completing a record-breaking come-from-behind perfomance to win the 2017 IRONMAN World Championship.

HONORING THE FINISH LINE

2017

Jan Frodeno came to the 2017 IRONMAN World Championship looking for his third consecutive title. He was already one of the most decorated triathletes of all time – he won the Olympic gold medal at the 2008 Beijing Games and two IRONMAN 70.3 World Championship titles alongside those two IRONMAN World Championship titles. He felt a great pressure to turn out a good performance, not only from within, but from his peers and fans. At first, it looked like he was going to do it. He made a good exit from the water, though he wasn't in the lead. By mile 76 of the bike race he was in the top pack but, as he came off his bike to start on the marathon, the element of the event at which he should have been strongest, a back injury flared up. Frodeno immediately realized his chance of another victory was gone. In excruciating pain, Frodeno was forced to the ground where he laid down for over 30 minutes. Once he was able to get back to his feet, he made the decision that, rather than give up, he would continue to walk the race. Patrick Lange won the race in a time of 8 hours 1 minute 40 seconds. Meanwhile, determined Frodeno finished the event, ending up in 35th position with an overall time of 9 hours 15 minutes 44 seconds. Of that, the marathon had taken him 4 hours 1 minute 57 seconds. His refusal to quit created a gracious, powerful image and a moment that represents the essence of every athlete at the start line of an IRONMAN event – making it to the finish!

▶ Jan Frodeno couldn't quite leap across the finish line as he had done the year before, but his determination to reach the finish line and gracious acknowledgement of the crowd exemplified the IRONMAN spirit.

IRONMAN
LEGENDS

Ever since the very first race in 1978, IRONMAN® has been about showcasing the incredible athletes who take part in, and overcome, the events, pushing themselves to new limits in the process. Their stories – whether of the many hours they spend dedicated to training, the sheer determination to finish, or their ability to dig deep for an extra ounce of energy when the going gets tough – are an inspiration to every potential IRONMAN athlete. This chapter contains ten interviews with eleven true IRONMAN legends, illustrating these stories in their own words.

◄ Daniela Ryf, biking her way to victory at the 2015 IRONMAN 70.3 Bahrain, months after winning her first IRONMAN World Championship.

JOHN AND JUDY COLLINS

Nationality:

Honors:
1998 – IRONMAN Hall of Fame inductee

BIOGRAPHY
U.S. Navy Commander John Collins and his wife Judy were stationed in Honolulu in the late 1970s when the idea for the IRONMAN® triathlon originated. It came about after a fruitful discussion at an awards ceremony in February 1977, during which the Collins family developed a way to settle the age-old dispute about which athletes were the fittest: runners, swimmers or cyclists. IRONMAN triathlon was born.

The Collinses organized the event for the first two years, making finishers' shirts and even the original trophy themselves, before John was posted elsewhere and the "race box" – a shoe box with race applications and notes – was handed over to Valerie Silk. Since then, the whole family (John, Judy, sons and daughters alike) have all completed IRONMAN events and they are still honored at each and every IRONMAN World Championship race to this day.

IRONMAN co-founders John and Judy Collins's interview with Bob Babbitt

BB: What was the discussion that led to the creation of the IRONMAN triathlon?

Judy C: "Here's what happened. We came back from competing in the San Diego Track Club Triathlon; we thought it had been fun. We showed back up at our swim practice and we told our swim coach about it. He put on the first Coronado Optimist Club Triathlon, which he designed for the swimmers. It was only a one-mile run."

John C: "The discussion was always that the swimmers thought the swim should be longer, and the runners thought the swim was too long. We didn't have many biking friends."

In terms of coming up with the whole concept of IRONMAN triathlons, John, was that something that you announced to the group?

John C: "No. We were both there [at an awards night]. Judy, at one end of the table, was having this normal discussion about what should the distances be. How many steps would it take to be equivalent to the number of strokes in the water, that sort of thing. I'm at the other end of the table not paying any attention to it

at all. I was talking to these other guys about something I had read about called oxygen uptake, now called VO2 Max, and why that was the best measure of the athletic ability of distance or endurance athletes."

Judy C: "John heard the word bicycle and, all of a sudden, he dropped into the conversation."

John C: "It hit me that we had the three events [in Hawai`i]. We had the Waikiki Roughwater Swim, and we had the Honolulu Marathon, and the around-the-island bicycle race, which was about 115 miles. It looked like if we cut about three miles off that bike ride we could finish the ride at Aloha Tower, where the Honolulu Marathon started."

Isn't that funny.

John C: "This was all paced off of a Hertz rental car map, with two fingers, on a table."

Where did the term 'IRONMAN' come from?

Judy C: "When we decided to make a logo."

John C: "In the beginning I had said the gun would go off and whoever finishes first we'll call him the 'IRONMAN.' That was in reference to a guy from the shipyard. Everyone called him the Ironman because he ran a 7:32-per mile pace and he could do one mile or 10 miles or 50 miles at that same pace."

John, you made the original IRONMAN trophies, correct?

John C: "Yes. My idea was to weld together some bolts and it turns out that I wasn't as good of a welder as I thought I was, so I ended up in desperation soldering them out of copper plate and copper tubing. I was still working on that a couple of days before the event. This is not an easy solder job to do, which is why about half the heads have fallen off over the years."

Which actually is appropriate. You need to have a hole in your head to do an IRONMAN triathlon race.

John C: "What we didn't have was a lot of money, or any kind of sponsorship."

I think you lost $25 in the first year?

John C: "Pretty much. Just about $25 and it cost you $3 to enter."

And then the following year, you struck it rich. You made $25, so you were even after two years. You guys are financial geniuses.

John C: "How many race promoters do you

know who broke even in two years?"

Fifteen people started the race in 1978?

John C: "18 showed up and 15 started."

When people think about events nowadays, they're thinking aid stations, they're thinking bike racks, they're thinking of all that stuff. We're talking none of the above at those early IRONMAN events. Roads aren't blocked off and you had your own crew all day long to support you.

Judy C: "You had to have a support team, and that support team provided your food and beverages. We provided the electrolyte drink, and you carried dimes with you."

The dimes were for emergency phone calls?

Judy C: "No, required phone calls. You had to call in from the public phone booths around the island."

John C: "When you reached certain points, your support team was required to call in and say, 'This is so and so and I'm in Haleiwa and John Dunbar just passed here.'"

What was the attraction of an IRONMAN race?

John C: "We hit a new demographic. 'I'm gonna try something I haven't done before just for the hell of it', but there was another group of people, of whom there are now many. They were people that were going through their own life crises and saw this as a chance to make a new life: 'If I could only do this, then everything will be all right.'"

Judy C: "It certainly helped that it was in Honolulu."

When you look at IRONMAN races now, there are 41 IRONMAN events, and over 110 IRONMAN 70.3® races. They have events all over the world, they even have IRONKIDS® races… did you have any sense that this thing could become such a juggernaut?

Judy C: "We didn't have that kind of imagination, but what we did know at the time was, anecdotally, we always ran faster if we swam beforehand. We swam faster if the car didn't start and we'd had to race five miles on the bike to the swim start. We were getting faster every time we went out… We didn't know the word cross-training, but that's what we were doing. So in that way, it's not."

Before we finish up, I need you to recite the "Swim 2.4 miles. Bike 112 miles. Run 26.2 miles. Brag for the rest of your life!" IRONMAN motto.

Judy C: "When there was a break in the awards that night, John came back to the table. It was very noisy and he leaned over and in my ear he said what he's about to say now."

John C: "Well, it came from the wife of a friend of ours who we had talked into doing the marathon. She said, 'The rule is that you cannot brag about anything for longer than it took you to do it.'"

I'm not sure I like that.

Judy C: "That's why we chafed against that, because we saw telling stories as the fourth event."

Judy C: "We decided that if you completed this event, the IRONMAN triathlon, you would never have to stop talking about it."

John C: "It was actually in one of the handout sheets for the first event, and it said, 'Swim 2.4 miles. Bike 112 miles. Run 26.2 miles. Brag for the rest of your life!'"

▼ IRONMAN co-founders John and Judy Collins at the 25th anniversary event in Kailua-Kona in 2003.

GORDON HALLER

Date of Birth: August 24, 1950
Nationality:

Honors:
1978 – IRONMAN World Championship, first place
2003 – IRONMAN Hall of Fame inductee

BIOGRAPHY
Gordon Haller was the winner of the very first IRONMAN World Championship in 1978, finishing in a time of 11:46:40. A training fanatic, Haller would work overtime five days a week in order to be able to have extra time to swim, bike, and run. In the two weeks before the first IRONMAN race, he tapered his training schedule down... but still ran 187 miles, biked 30 miles, and swam 8,000 meters! Still active in the world of triathlon 40 years later, he was inducted into the IRONMAN Hall of Fame in 2003.

Gordon Haller's interview before the 40th Anniversary of the first race in 2018 with Bob Babbitt

BB: So you've done 17 IRONMAN races in Hawai`i, right?
GH: "This year will be my 18th in Hawai`i and 24th overall."

What was the entry fee for that first IRONMAN race?
"Five bucks."

Five bucks?
"You got a refund on it, too, because they didn't use the whole five bucks. So it ended up being about two or three dollars."

On race day, you've got John Dunbar there, who's a Navy SEAL. You come out of the water about 20-minutes behind Dunbar. Did you have a sense of where you were compared to the other guys?
"Only because Hank [Haller's team manager] told me about it. He said, 'You're about 20 minutes behind Dunbar, and you're in eighth place out of 15,' so I was the exact middle guy and had a 1:19 swim. Sometimes it's listed as 1:20, but I call 1:19. I took the usual long transition running through the hotel to the locker room and showered and changed into my bike gear."

You went in and showered?
"Most of us did that because we didn't want to be all salty. It was more like the shower you take when you've been swimming at the beach."

Did you have bike shoes?
"I wore my marathon running shoes. They had no cushion at all, but that's what I ran a 2:27 in because they didn't weigh anything, but they also worked fine as a bike shoe. I still have those in a box. I actually have all of those things that I wore that day in a box."

You end up with a 6:56 bike ride with no roads blocked off. Did you try to follow traffic rules, or were you like, look, okay, there's no cars coming. Let's go.
"We were told to follow traffic rules and I pretty much do that anyway, but if there's nobody around on the North Shore, you go for it."

What did you eat during that race?
"Bananas, orange slices, chocolate chip cookies. We also had Gookinaid, ERG. My secret weapon was protein sparing. You take the amino acids so that your body doesn't eat up the protein in your muscles when you get a long way into the race and you run out of fats and carbohydrates."

You were way ahead of the curve in terms of understanding the science of the sport.
"I did a lot of studying."

Do you know what place you were in off the bike?
"I had the fastest bike ride."

Knowing that you're a 2:27 marathoner and you're, what, 12 minutes back at the end of the bike...
"Yep, I was 12 minutes behind and my personal record was 12 minutes better than John's."

So you knew it could be a tight one. Was your crew giving you some reports on where he was?
"Not really. I was about 12 miles in before they spotted him. I caught him at 15, but I got a cramp in my hamstrings, so I had to stop and get a massage, and then I caught him again at 18 and then I had to go to bathroom, so I stopped at the Porta-John there. Then, I caught him again at 20 and got another cramp. Then, I caught him at 21 and I was thinking I was still going as fast as he was with all those stops, so all I had to do was not stop and I would beat him. When I caught him at 21, he looked really bad. His face was all white."

He was wobbling.
"He looked at me like, 'Go ahead, shoot me now,' and I was starting to feel really good at that point. I had a couple guys join with me and run the last five miles. One of them carried

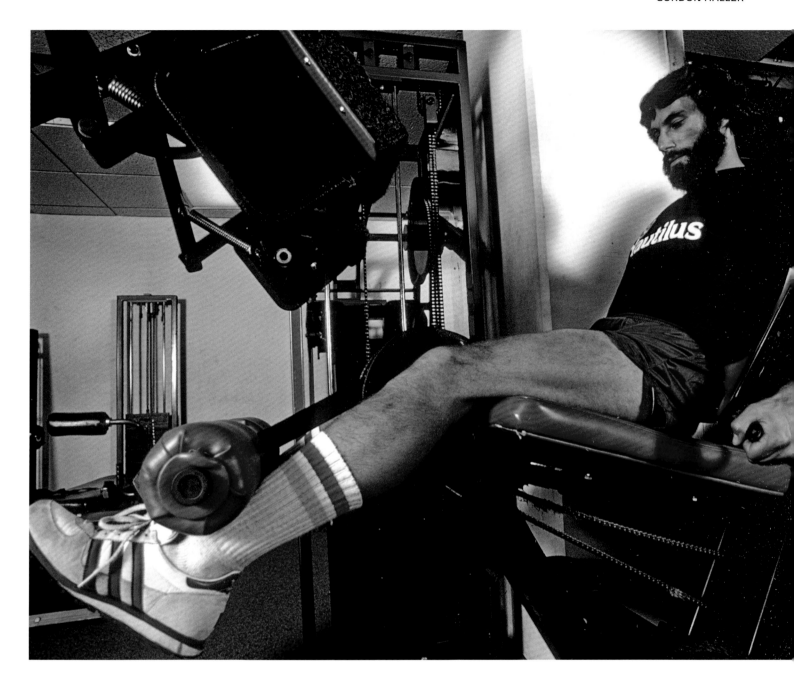

a water bottle with water in it and the other one carried a bottle of de-fizzed cola. I just hammered the last 5.2 miles in 30 minutes."

You go 11:46. He goes 12:20. You're coming to the finish of this amazing event. When you come across the line after winning the first IRONMAN race in Kapiolani Park, is anybody there?

"Yeah, there were a couple of guys sitting in lawn chairs and one guy says, 'Are you in the race?' and I said, 'Yeah,' and he says, 'Well, you're done.'"

You win in 1978 and then Sports Illustrated comes over in 1979. It was Dunbar against Haller. Did you feel that going into the 1979 race?

"Yes and no. John and I were friends, so it was a friendly rivalry kind of thing. We wanted to beat each other, of course. I kind of screwed up that year. I over-trained and I did a 33-mile run the week before the second IRONMAN triathlon. I got a sinus infection and that kind of weakened me a little bit. But I still had the fastest run in that year's IRONMAN race. The swim was brutal in 1979. We had six-foot swells and 40-knot winds, and I'm not a swimmer. When I came out of the water in 1:15:59, Hank asks me if I want to quit and I said, 'Are you kidding? The hard part's over. I just have to ride 112 miles and run a marathon.'"

▲ Gordon Haller in the weight room preparing to defend his title at the 1979 IRONMAN World Championship.

PAULA NEWBY-FRASER

Date of Birth: June 2, 1962
Nationality:

Honors:
1985 – IRONMAN World Championship, third place
1986 – IRONMAN World Championship, first place
1987 – IRONMAN World Championship, third place
1988 – IRONMAN World Championship, first place
1989 – IRONMAN World Championship, first place
1990 – IRONMAN World Championship, second place
1991 – IRONMAN World Championship, first place
1992 – IRONMAN World Championship, first place
1993 – IRONMAN World Championship, first place
1994 – IRONMAN World Championship, first place
1996 – IRONMAN World Championship, first place
1996 – IRONMAN Hall of Fame inductee

BIOGRAPHY
Paula Newby-Fraser, also known as "The Queen of Kona," is the most successful IRONMAN athlete of all time. She won the IRONMAN World Championship race a total of eight times over the course of a decade, breaking record after record along the way. In 1988, she produced what has been called the finest endurance performance of all time to finish eleventh overall in the race – out of both men and women! Her final course record was so far ahead of the field that it took until 2009 for another athlete to break it. Newby-Fraser was inducted into the IRONMAN Hall of Fame after her final victory in 1996.

Paula Newby-Fraser's interview with Bob Babbitt

BB: Your first time to Kona was in 1985 and you finished third. After getting third, was there a lot of excitement?
PNF: "You know, it was great. In South Africa doing well in sports is tremendously celebrated, so it was a huge deal in South Africa."

Did you think at that point that you should be racing triathlons as a career? Because in 1985 there was no prize money for Kona.
"On my way home from Hawai`i, I stopped in San Diego. I got to look around and saw the lifestyle that they were living there while pursuing triathlon. At that point I thought it might be something you could do as a living."

So 1986 was a pivotal year. You come over to Kona, but you're not first across the line.
"I was on the run course and they said, 'Patricia's been disqualified but she's not leaving the course.' And I thought, well none of that matters. I've just got to get on with it. So when I saw the finish tape, I was not 100 per cent sure [I had won], but either way I didn't care. I felt like it was a great race and the time was a shock. I never could have imagined going 9:49 and taking over 35 minutes off of the course record."

The first time out in 1985 you went 10:31!
"The first time I went to Kona I had never ridden 112 miles and I'd never run a marathon, so it was all new territory for me. But still, sub 10

hours seemed amazing to me."

So you won in 1986, but it was one of those things where people wondered if it was just because Patricia got disqualified rather than you winning. When you go back the following year, now there's this New Zealander named Erin Baker on the start list. She went 9:35, taking another 14 minutes off of the course record.
"To be honest with you, I was really disappointed after 1987. I won in 1986 and I went back in 1987 feeling the pressure to show that I was a champion. I needed to race well to prove to myself that the year before was not a fluke. So that loss in 1987, so late into the race, that really motivated me.

"I went away and decided to stay in San Diego. That's when there was a very big shift for me in how I was committing myself to triathlon and what it was to me. That race gave me pause and made me think, 'Well you know what, why don't I try to make a career out of this?' Not just one foot in, one foot out."

When you look at it, you went 9:49 in 1986 and Erin goes 9:35 in 1987. In 1988 you finished eleventh overall [men and women] and go 9:01:01. How reaffirming was that?
"That winter I sat down and started thinking about what a consistent training program looked like. I didn't have a coach, so I looked at Mark Allen and Scott Molina and Scott Tinley to see what they were doing. Probably the greatest influence in my training mindset was Professor Tim Noakes from South Africa. He had always

said to me, 'Whatever you do, try and get by on the least amount of training you possibly can.' By using a little bit of Tim Noakes's being under-trained philosophy, and also looking at the consistency of the athletes around me, I started to figure out what would work.

"I wasn't sure what was possible. As was always my tradition, I never raced with a watch. So 1988 was a shock for me as well. All I did was put my head down and go."

Erin Baker gets second that year and she went 20 minutes faster than she did the year before. Erin's not there in 1989 and you win again. In 1990 she wins and you're second. Then you win and she's second. Did you and Erin ever discuss that whole era?

"You know, there wasn't really a relationship. It was tough. But for all the negative and the positive, her attitude drove me – probably more than I would acknowledge at the time."

To me the mark of a champion is coming back after a major disappointment and winning again. You lose your big lead and your chance for that eighth title in 1995 and I remember talking to you leading into the 1996 race. You were racing a rookie, Natascha Badmann, who'd go on to win the IRONMAN World Championship six times. Take me through your mindset going into that race.

"After the 1995 race, where I came apart, I walked away from the sport and took a breather. I got a better perspective. It's a great sport. I really loved it. Prize money, no prize money, none of it mattered. I was just back to loving what I did. I got a bit of speed back and so when I went to Kona in 1996, I was like, I can handle this. Then I got out on the bike and I got a penalty in the first ten miles.

"I didn't get flustered. I rode myself to the front of the race, got off the bike, and sat in the penalty tent. I watched Karen Smyers and Natascha Badmann come off the bike and go out on the run. And I'm like, 'Oh, well. This is what I'm dealt.'"

Then there's a point during the marathon where you're side-by-side with Natascha Badmann and in past years that might have been a problem. But it seemed like it was almost as if you enjoyed that.

"Natascha took off and dropped me going into the Natural Energy Lab. She was running and knew I couldn't match her speed at that point. There's nothing I could do, so I was just going to settle in and grind the pace that I knew I could maintain. She was a rookie and probably set a pace that she couldn't maintain. Once I caught

▲ When Paula Newby-Fraser was racing in the IRONMAN World Championship, it was almost a certainty that she would be out in the lead, as she was here in 1993.

up to her and I was running with her, I knew that I could beat her."

Was that your most satisfying win after what happened the year before?

"For sure. I learned a lot about mindset going into that race. Doing IRONMAN races, you make the choice to do it, and it can overwhelm you if you don't know why it is that you're out there and what drives you. It's important, because if you know what drives you, you can get the best out of yourself and the best out of the day."

DAVE SCOTT

Date of Birth: January 4, 1954
Nationality:

Honors:
1980 – IRONMAN World Championship, first place
1982 – IRONMAN World Championship (February),
second place
IRONMAN World Championship (October), first
place
1983 – IRONMAN World Championship, first place
1984 – IRONMAN World Championship, first place
1986 – IRONMAN World Championship, first place
1987 – IRONMAN World Championship, first place
1989 – IRONMAN World Championship, second place
1993 – IRONMAN Hall of Fame inductee
1994 – IRONMAN World Championship, second place

BIOGRAPHY
Dave Scott's six victories in the IRONMAN World Championship means that "The Man," as he is affectionately known, ties with long-time rival Mark Allen as the male athlete to have won the race the most times ever. Their duels throughout the formative years of IRONMAN's history helped shape the sport, never more so than when they both broke Dave Scott's own course record during the Iron War of 1989.

In 1993, he became the first person to be inaugurated into the IRONMAN Hall of Fame, appropriate recognition for a man whose intensity, competitiveness and extraordinary athletic ability embodied the qualities that IRONMAN racing represents.

Dave Scott's interview with Bob Babbitt

BB: When did you hear about the IRONMAN races?
DS: "I read the article in *Sports Illustrated* in 1979. I had competed in the Waikiki Roughwater Swim, the 2.4-mile swim that kicked off the IRONMAN triathlon, so I was very familiar with doing the longer swims and decided to commit to the race in January 1980.

I did a mock triathlon on my own. There was a century bike ride in my town, so I got up in the morning and swam 5,000 meters before riding the 100-miler, and I had kind of mapped out a 20-mile run. So I finished that 20-mile run and said, 'I feel pretty good.' I think I did it on a glass of water... I was a little bit dehydrated."

I remember talking to Jim Lampley, the ABC commentator for the 1980 IRONMAN World Championship. At the time, everybody was talking about John Howard, the three-time Olympian. And I remember Jim telling me, "I sat down with this guy Dave Scott and said, so you were a NCAA champion swimmer, and he's like, 'No, no.' Were you an Olympic cyclist? 'No.' Were you a runner? 'Not really.'"

"Yeah, Jim was a little dismayed. He thought that he had been misled about the talent pool."

After you saw the time that Tom Warren had done to win the 1979 IRONMAN World Championship did you have a sense that, "You know, I think I can go faster than that"?

"In that interview with Jim, he did say, 'Are you going to get through this race?' As if sort of challenging me, and I think I was a little bit irritated by that. And I said, 'I am going to race this event.' But I had no idea who John Howard was, nor any of the other competitors."

So you are a 26-year-old swim instructor from Davis, California, and you won this race. Did it change anything for you?

"Not much changed at all at the time. Life goes on. I didn't really feel as though anything would happen."

1983 was a classic race. You end up winning by 33 seconds over Scott Tinley and at the finish you had nothing left. What do you remember about that race?

"The lead evaporated quickly. I had about two and a half minutes with five miles to go on Scott. Those of you that have run the race know that at that point you're not really quite sure what your first name is, let alone what course you're on. I was starting to really focus on just one step after another. It finally came down to that last mile. I heard that he was under a minute behind. I won by 33 seconds and if I'd had another 65 feet to run, I think Scott would have won."

1984 is really the first battle with Mark Allen, right? He had a big lead of 12 minutes off the bike.

"I don't know if I was overly confident when starting to run with that 12-minute deficit, but I felt good. My thought at the time was, 'Mark is beginning to die, I'm feeling great.' So when I came out on the run, without doing the math, I thought 'just be consistent and be aggressive at the beginning.'"

You catch Mark Allen about halfway through the marathon and win your fourth title. In 1986, you win and he finishes second. He basically shadowed you throughout the day. But, in 1987, things changed.

"I just think because Mark seemingly was really invincible at all different distances, there was more tension then. He was an incredible competitor. He could race the Olympic distance or a half-distance, but he had trouble at the IRONMAN World Championship. In 1987, I knew it was going to be a closer battle."

Mark got ahead. He had about a five-minute lead in the run. And then you caught him on the way back. And I love the stealth move.

"Mark was on the far left-hand side. His van was on his right, kind of in the middle of the road. Mine was on my left. I decided to take the far right side so the two runners were on opposite sides of the road, with two vehicles in between. They did catch that on ABC's *Wide World of Sports* and they actually said, 'Here's Dave Scott slipping by unannounced.' I didn't want him to shadow me. I probably would have started crying and fallen to the road."

In 1988, you pull out the night before the race with a knee issue. That really set up 1989.

"I knew the stakes were higher. I felt — based on an early season race that we did in Australia together where I actually ran very, very well and Mark went roaring by me — he would be ready to go."

You and Mark swam within a second of each other and then rode within a second of each other. Throughout the marathon you were side by side.

"It was an epic day. There were several times that I felt great on the bike and I said, 'I'm going to drop Mark, I'm going to go really hard.' And I knew that he was kind of like a rubber band behind me, that he would close that gap and it would come down to the run.

"We went out very, very fast for the first eight miles and then slowed down. And with the old turn-around with 10 miles to go, we quickened the pace again. I had a tactic that if we were together when we got to the top of Palani Hill that my unsightly form would be favorable going down the hill. But Mark's tactic was to make the move at the base of the hill. He made his move and for all those little steps that he was taking, I was losing about three or four inches. When we got to the top of that hill he had 35 seconds on me."

So you finish that race and you have to be a little conflicted. You've just taken 18 minutes off your course record, but you didn't win your seventh title. How hard was that for you?

"I think about that race. There's a lot of shoulda, coulda, woulda's, but I tell athletes that I coach now that you have to be spontaneous in the moment. Don't second-guess. On that particular day, it turned out to be an incredible battle."

Unfortunately, you were injured in 1990, 1991, 1992 and 1993. I tell people all the time, what might have been your greatest race was coming back in 1994 at the age of 40. People thought you were done. Right?

"It was a big day. I was still very passionate about doing this sport. Over the previous five years, my two boys were born and my commitment to the sport was still the same, but I had other concerns in life. That particular day, I was with Greg Welch throughout the bike, but I didn't feel good at the outset of the run. He ended up winning by about three minutes. But it was a good day."

It was a great day.

▼ At the age of 40, Dave Scott still challenged hard for the IRONMAN World Championship in 1994, finishing in a well-deserved second place.

MARK ALLEN

Date of Birth: January 12, 1958
Nationality:

Honors:
1983 – IRONMAN World Championship, third place
1986 – IRONMAN World Championship, second place
1987 – IRONMAN World Championship, second place
1989 – IRONMAN World Championship, first place
1990 – IRONMAN World Championship, first place
1991 – IRONMAN World Championship, first place
1992 – IRONMAN World Championship, first place
1993 – IRONMAN World Championship, first place
1995 – IRONMAN World Championship, first place
1997 – IRONMAN Hall of Fame inductee

BIOGRAPHY
Mark Allen's "Iron War" rivalry with Dave Scott defined the early years of the IRONMAN World Championship race. He took seven attempts to cross the finish line in first – winning for the first time in 1989 – but once he did he was never defeated in Kona again.

Allen eventually became a six-time IRONMAN World Champion, tying Dave Scott as the most successful male IRONMAN athlete of all time. His final victory came in 1995 at the age of 37, making him the oldest male IRONMAN World Champion at the time. He was inducted into the IRONMAN Hall of Fame in 1997.

Mark Allen's interview with Bob Babbitt

BB: You go to the 1982 IRONMAN World Championship. I remember watching the ABC coverage, and they knew so little about you I think they had your name A-L-L-A-N on the chyron [electronically generated caption] below. But you ride up to Dave Scott. He's the legend.
MA: "Unbelievable. He was the 'IRONMAN.' I was blown away. I thought, how can I be with the best guy in the world? But let me enjoy this. I pedaled up to him. I like to goof around. I said, 'Hey, Dave, when we're done with the bike, you want to go for a run?' He looked at me like I was insane, and he asked what my name was. I told him, and he goes, 'Oh, yeah, I've heard of you,' and he pulled away.

"I thought, 'Okay, well, conversation with the champ is over.' I went to shift my bike into a bigger gear, and that's when my first bit of IRONMAN mishap happened. My derailleur broke, and my chain just slid over into the biggest gear. My race was done."
In 1983, you get third. Then, in 1984, you out-split Dave on the bike but he caught you in a run. That was the beginning of the Dave Scott vs Mark Allen rivalry.
"That was a rough one. Like you said, I came off the bike pretty far ahead of everybody. I think I had almost 12 minutes by the time I left transition. I was high-fiving people because I thought, 'I've got this thing.' At the bottom of Palani Road, I was thinking, 'I'm going to be the IRONMAN World champion.' When I got to

the top of it, about five minutes later, I felt like every ounce of energy had just dripped out of my body. It was pretty disappointing, because it was a hard lesson, but one that I needed to learn: clearly, an IRONMAN race is not over until you cross the finish line."
1986 was an interesting year. You had just won the Nice triathlon. You only had a couple of weeks in between. I remember when you came over to Kona there wasn't quite the tension between Mark Allen and Dave Scott that I saw the following year.
"My focus that year was to win the Nice triathlon. I wasn't even going to compete at the IRONMAN World Championship race. I was still recovering. I was never in it with Dave. I think he knew that there's just no way that you can do Nice and then, two weeks later, come back and truly be vying for the championship at Kona. He felt pretty invincible, and he had reason to feel that way."
In 1987, the tension was there.
"I think he wanted to win that year for a number of reasons. Many more reasons than any of the other years."
You get a four- or five-minute lead in the run, and Dave goes by and wins his sixth and final IRONMAN World Championship title.
"Yeah. It was a rough day for me. When I woke up that morning, my stomach, my intestines, were all knotted up. With 10 miles to go, I had a five-minute gap. I had been pulling away. But, unfortunately, a couple of miles later, I knew that something was

really, really wrong. I was forced to walk. Dave ended up passing me. I finished in second and realized that I had some internal bleeding going on. I went to the hospital and that night they put tubes everywhere."

Oh my God. Talk a little bit about Brant Secunda and shamanism.

"One of the things that Brant [Secunda] really helps people develop is a relationship with nature, and to feel comfortable, no matter where they are. That was a huge missing piece for me in the World Championship. I was not comfortable in Kona when I was there to race. I was intimidated by the natural environment there, which is very intense. Secunda really helped me with that, and I made a connection with him prior to the 1989 race. It was the first year that I was in Kona, and just feeling like, 'I love this place.'"

Dave went 8:10 and was 18 minutes faster than his course record. You guys took the race to another level. When you were still together late in the race, did you have a place where you wanted to make your move?

"Yeah. I knew that if we got to the top of the hill together, that he would have the race, because he was definitely faster than me on the downhills. When we got to the very bottom of the last uphill that was going to lead to that, that's where I went. Something just said, 'Go', and I started to sprint, as best as you can sprint in an IRONMAN race. When I got to the bottom of the hill in town to make the left, I looked back, and I couldn't see him. That was the first time when all of a sudden, I knew I had it. Nothing was going to happen. I wasn't going to cramp. He wasn't going to catch me. It was just amazing. One minute, I had the biggest smile on my face, and the next minute, I had these tears coming down my cheeks, because it was just a very intense moment."

After you beat Dave, you win in 1990, 1991, 1992 and 1993. I tell people I think one of the greatest races I've ever seen – besides 1989 – was 1995, because you were 37 years old, had been away for a year, and getting off the bike you're 13 minutes back. What was going through your mind?

"I'm thinking, 'Impossible.' There's no way. Nobody had closed that big of a gap to be the champion. A couple miles into the marathon, I was passing the entrance to my condo, and I was feeling pretty rotten at that point. I thought, 'Oh, that would just be so easy. Just go down there, go get a shower. You've won five of these things.' But finally, after about a mile of running, I was able to get my mind to be quiet, and something said, 'Just take it to the finish. Just get to that finish line. This is your final IRONMAN race. You got into this sport to cross the finish line. This is the last one. Get there.' Suddenly, it felt like the whole world of opportunity began to open back up."

You end up running 2:42, and catch Thomas at around 23 miles and win by 2 minutes and 25 seconds. You've just put together one of the greatest comebacks in history. I'm sure that because you know you're not coming back, the emotions must have been pretty raw.

"To win that race, it took way more than it took to beat Dave in 1989. I had to find those 1,001-reasons why it was important to keep going and give it everything I had. When I was coming down to the finish, I was filled up. I knew that was the best race I could ever possibly have. I was fortunate that it happened on a day where I said, 'This is going to be it.'"

GRAHAM FRASER

Date of Birth: June 21, 1961
Nationality:

Honors:
2012 – IRONMAN Hall of Fame inductee

BIOGRAPHY
Graham Fraser became the sixteenth IRONMAN Hall of Fame inductee in 2012, in recognition of the many years of service he had provided for the sport. Inspired by competing in the IRONMAN World Championship race in 1985, he returned to his hometown of Grimsby, Ontario, with the plan of founding his own triathlon series, before taking over the organization of the IRONMAN Canada event in 1996. Buoyed by his success, Fraser was later instrumental in the expansion of IRONMAN throughout North America and, eventually, the world.

Graham Fraser's interview with Bob Babbitt

BB: IRONMAN Canada had been in Penticton but it was hurting financially. And you came in and basically saved that event I think.
GF: "Well, I don't think I was the one who saved the event. The entry fees had all disappeared and the event was going down the wrong path. It was in crisis mode. I went to see David Yates, President of IRONMAN at that time. He was pushing me to take over IRONMAN Canada. I said, 'Look, I'll put the money in, I'll do it, I'll take the risk, but I don't want you to start putting on IRONMAN events everywhere and put me out of business. So why don't you just do this: if there's going to be any events in North America, I have the rights to them.'

"And David at the time didn't think they were going to do any events in North America so they signed that."
At that point, there was the IRONMAN World Championship in Hawai'i and IRONMAN Canada, and there were other IRONMAN events around the world. But there were no other IRONMAN races in the rest of the U.S. For you to have the vision to understand that this thing was going to grow is pretty amazing.
"I could feel it. When you live and breathe a sport and you do it every day, you kind of get a sense of where it might go. But we weren't

sure. And then, when we started Lake Placid..."
Yeah, so how did that come about?
"Penticton started to sell out and do well. We brought in sponsors, we brought in TV. The athletes started coming, and they were sleeping in sleeping bags to register for the race at that point. I went to the IRONMAN organization and said, 'Look there's a need for another race here.' Our friend Kevin McKinnon had spent a lot of time in Lake Placid and he suggested that we go there first. It was an unbelievable venue.

"I went to the mayor, and he called a meeting with all the officials. I started doing my little dog and pony show about what IRONMAN triathlon is, and literally within five minutes the mayor stands up, pounds his fist on the table and says, 'We're doing it.' That was it.

"And then we started talking about the planning and what we needed to do to get the venues, and this and that. And there was no permit process back then. They actually said, 'Well, we don't have permits, you just write up something and we'll sign it.'

"Five days later, we signed a contract. We announced the event five days later... it was all in fives. Five days later, it was full."
It was sold out?
"Sold out. That's when Lew Friedland [president of the IRONMAN organization] and I then went back and I said, there is something here. He said, 'we better get another one going.' That became IRONMAN Florida. I started looking for a venue right away. We didn't even have any staff, by the way. We didn't have people to put these events on. We had five people. That's all you did, all day every day, was pull off those events."
When you look at your formula, it's all about heads in beds. IRONMAN Coeur d'Alene, IRONMAN Lake Placid and IRONMAN Florida, what's great about those communities is that they're all places that have hotels, they're all destination communities. But they're also small enough for an IRONMAN race to dominate while the event is in town. Is that what you looked for?
"There are a few things that we looked for. First of all, the most important thing is that the swim, bike and run have to work. And in my mind it had to be like an A-grade swim, A-grade

bike and A-grade run. You don't want to swim in places people don't want to swim.

"And then you want to be in communities that you would want to go to, like, 'Would I want to take my family there for vacation?' And you want to feel like you own the place. I'll never forget driving around Lake Placid that first year and driving by the arena. I was in the lead car and it felt like the Tour de France with all of the spectators. That's what athletes want. That's awesome!"

As a guy who has done over 300 triathlons, how did that factor into your success growing the IRONMAN brand?

"Your personal experiences lead to a lot of decisions in your life. And not just being an athlete, but when you're an athlete, you're hanging around athletes. So, you've got this feedback from all the people that you train with, and you sense what they like and don't like. Just being in that environment was a huge help. We believed in the pre- and post-race banquets to help create this atmosphere of specialness. I remember being at the Kona Surf Hotel back in 1984 at the IRONMAN Banquet. That made a

huge impression on me.

"I was 22 years old and I was glossy-eyed at seeing Dave Scott up there on stage and all of the best triathletes all gathered in this one spot. It gave me this energy to do my event. That's why it was very important when we developed the whole business model to have banquets with great videos and inspirational stories.

"And of course, the most important part of all is to make sure you have a great swim, bike and run course. If you screw up swim, bike, run, nothing else matters. So you have to find those courses that are safe and have all those little characteristics that an athlete would want.

"When you put your name on an event, like our generation of race directors has, it has to be great. It's your pride, it's your name. You're not a hidden entity that no one knows; you're the entity. They know your face, they know your name, and they're going to find you. So, you have your pride on the line. I set a high, high standard. That sounds arrogant, but when someone did my races, I wanted them to walk away and say, when I go to his race, it's always the best race."

▲ The plaque on the shores of Mirror Lake in Lake Placid, marking the home of the IRONMAN Lake Placid event that Fraser founded in 1989.

CHRISSIE WELLINGTON

Date of Birth: February 18, 1977
Nationality:

Honours:
2007 – IRONMAN World Championship, first place
2008 – IRONMAN World Championship, first place
2009 – IRONMAN World Championship, first place
2011 – IRONMAN World Championship, first place
　　　　Ultra Distance World Record Holder, 8:18:13
2017 – IRONMAN Hall of Fame inductee

BIOGRAPHY
After turning professional in 2007, Chrissie Wellington won the IRONMAN World Championship race at the first time of trying, becoming the first triathlete to win the event less than a year after turning professional.

It was a sign of things to come: over the 13 Ultra Distance races she would run over the course of her career, Chrissie would remain undefeated in every single one. She completed a hat-trick of victories in 2009 by breaking the course record at the IRONMAN World Championship that had been held by Paula Newby-Fraser for 17 years, before missing out in 2010 because of illness. Her return to Kailua-Kona, Hawai`i, in 2011 came after setting the Ultra Distance World Record in Germany in a time of 8:18:13, smashing the previous record by an incredible 32 minutes. However, a crash just two weeks before the race resulted in extensive injuries that led some to believe she should not even be on the start line. Once more, Chrissie showed her true champion spirit, triumphing against the odds before retiring in 2012 having run, as she herself said, her "perfect race".

Chrissie Wellington's interview with Bob Babbitt shortly after winning her fourth IRONMAN World Championship in 2011

BB: Chrissie, take us through your training this summer. Ten to twelve days before you head to Hawai`i, you had a crash.
CW: "Yeah, I mean I felt really strong in the lead-up to Kona. Two weeks prior to the race, I didn't realize that I had a flat front tire, and went to take a corner pretty fast. The next thing I know I'm on the ground. They rushed me off to the hospital, X-rayed everything and said that nothing was fractured, which was a huge relief."

At that point, did you feel like, "Oh my god, not again?" Because last year you got sick and weren't able to race.
"I think some of the words that I uttered are not for public consumption. But once they told me that nothing was broken, I was determined to race."

You were in the hospital for about six hours, four days before the most important race of the year, against Mirinda Carfrae, who's the defending World Champion. Was there a point where you started to think, "I don't know if I can make it to the starting line?"
"I always knew I'd be on the start line. Particularly after what happened last year. I think my concern was not being able to do myself justice. I tried to have faith in my body, and in particular in my mind to be strong and to be able to overcome the adversity.

"I do firmly believe in the strength of the human mind and the human spirit. I'd never suffered so much during a race as I did last weekend, yet, somehow, I managed to pull through and give a performance that I'm incredibly proud of."

So let's go through the race itself...
"I was nervous. I spoke to my coach Dave Scott the night before the race and he said, 'Look, no heroics in the swim. If you have to go slower than normal, then go slower than normal, because it's better to do that than to crush yourself and not be able to complete the race.'"

You went 1:01 for the swim, and it set up a great story. When you saw the clock coming out, were you like, "Oh my god, I can't believe I was 1:01 and I'm usually, like, 54?"
"I try not to dwell too much on things. I always try and stay in the moment, and try and keep a positive perspective."

How did you feel early on in the bike?
"I felt pretty sluggish in the initial stages, but I didn't want to go out too strongly. I think I slowly crept up on them without ever really over-exerting myself to catch them."

What was fun to watch was that when the run started, you were still 20 minutes down. At that point, people were really concerned. Mirinda Carfrae, the 2010 IRONMAN World Champion and the best runner in the sport, is not far behind. To me, any time you have all the bruising you had, it's going to affect you more in the run more than anything else.

"Yeah – definitely, particularly in the latter stages. I tried to keep my form, and remain positive. My strategy was simple, and that was just to put as much space between myself and Mirinda as I possibly could, and obviously try and do my damnedest to eat away at those in front of me. I deliberately went out quite hard. I went through the half [marathon] in 1:22, which is the fastest I've ever gone through the half at Kona, by far. It was incredibly hot out there, and trying to get enough fluid on board was very difficult."

When you start to fade a little bit, do you try to take on more at the aid station? Have you ever walked on that course, like through an aid station?

"No. I'm no hero, but I've never walked on that course, or in any IRONMAN race. I see the advantage for some people, but I never want to disrupt my stride. I've never felt the need to walk. I have a tried and tested nutrition strategy. I know people try and grab what they can from aid stations. I'm a lot more methodical and strategic. I have one gel every 25 minutes, and the only other thing I take on is water."

No cola, no electrolytes. Nothing like that?

"No, they are in the gels. I'm basically taking on a gel, and I'm taking on as much water as I can at the aid station. I actually took to putting ice down my chest and then holding a couple of cubes in my hands, to keep cooler."

So when you're coming down Ali'i Drive, and you realize that you're going to win your fourth IRONMAN World Championship, did it mean more than the other wins?

"Every race I've ever done, every World Championship victory, means a huge amount to me for many different reasons, but this is the race I'm the most proud of. I gave it absolutely everything and I overcame more pain and more discomfort, more physical and mental anguish than I ever could have imagined in a race, and for that, yeah, this is the race I'm most proud of.

"I left everything out there. Everything. I could not have given more, and it was great to finally have a battle, to finally have a fight, to have to chase people down, to have people chasing me down, and to show people that you can overcome adversity. Defining what's possible is a truly wonderful, very empowering feeling."

What did you learn about yourself through this?

"Before every race I ever do, I write on my race

wristband, 'Never, ever give up.' I think that's what I've learned. In summary, to never give up. To keep your head when all about you are losing theirs. Not to doubt yourself. To try and remain confident. I've realized once again the power of the human spirit.

"There were times during that race when it would be all too easy to just listen to the voice that's on one shoulder whispering in your ear saying, just pull over to the side, this hurts too much.

"Then I've got the louder voice in my ear saying, push on, push on, push on. You can overcome it. Luckily, that voice in the other ear is much louder, preaching the self-belief and the self-confidence that comes from overcoming what you don't think is possible to overcome."

▲Chrissie Wellington's full-distance record in South Africa in April 2011. She would beat her own record for a third time later that year in July.

 JAN FRODENO

Date of Birth: August 18, 1981
Nationality: ▆▆▆▆▆

Honours:
2008 – Olympic Games Triathlon, first place
2014 – IRONMAN World Championship, third place
IRONMAN 70.3 World Championship, second place
2015 – IRONMAN World Championship, first place
IRONMAN 70.3 World Championship, first place
2016 – IRONMAN World Championship, first place
Ultra Distance World Record Holder, 7:35:39

BIOGRAPHY
A triathlon competitor from a young age, Jan Frodeno capitalized on youthful promise with a gold medal at the 2008 Olympic Games. It was only in 2013 that he switched to the longer form, where he found almost immediate success in the shape of a bronze medal in his first appearance at the IRONMAN World Championship after a strong 2:47:46 split in the run – the fastest of the event.

After recovering from a cycling injury, Frodeno won the IRONMAN 70.3 World Championship before making history as the first triathlete ever to win both the Olympic gold medal and the IRONMAN World Championship title. He defeated a strong field that included both the 2013 and 2014 IRONMAN World Champions, Frederik Van Lierde and Sebastian Kienle, although it was German compatriot Andreas Raelert who he held off to record his gold in Hawaïi.

In 2016, he was part of a German 1-2-3 at the IRONMAN World Championship race, finishing at the head of the pack once again after another strong performance in all three disciplines. However, it was earlier in the year, on July 17, 2016, in his home country of Germany, that he made his greatest mark on triathlon history by shaving more than five minutes off of the world record for the Ultra Distance, cutting the record time down to 7:35:39.

Jan Frodeno's interview with Bob Babbitt shortly after winning his second IRONMAN World Championship in 2016

BB: You make the Olympic team in 2008. It was Javier Gómez from Spain who was the overwhelming favorite, right? They were already planning the victory parade back in Spain.
JF: "They actually did; it was one of my biggest motivators when I heard he had already planned his party before the Olympics."

You trained for pretty much that whole year knowing the finish was going to come down to the last couple of hundred yards.
"That was Javier Gómez's only weakness, so that was really our only chance at trying to win. Go big or go home. That's how we prepared. We ended up together on the finishing straight. I was just really, really grateful at that moment that [the final sprint] had finally started. It was actually quite a relief."

Fortunately, because of all of that sprint work, you reacted quickly enough, winning the gold.
"Yeah. It was pretty surreal at first. You dream of this 1,000 times and then all of a sudden it becomes real, but you're not quite sure whether it is real or not."

How tough was the transition to IRONMAN?
"To be honest, the mental part was the easiest, because I really wanted to be there, I wanted to be good. I had a dream, I had a goal, and now it was all about finding a plan and figuring out how to get there and execute."

I remember reading something you said: "If you want to talk about what's terrifying, it is the last hour of an IRONMAN race, because you're trying to get to the finish line but you don't know if you can get there."
"Yeah, absolutely: 2.4 miles of swimming, 112 miles of biking, and 26.2 miles of running. That in itself is pretty terrifying. It's not like, 'Wow, this is going to be an awesome day.' Really, it's always about perspective. Then you set your mind, you get the positive thoughts going, break it down into small pieces and make it manageable."

2015 was one of those classic years. You win IRONMAN Frankfurt, and the IRONMAN World Championship.
"My coach and I managed to work out a formula of consistency. We realized that it wasn't about putting in the big weeks. My record training week is somewhere around 49 hours, with 17 miles of swimming, 430 miles on the bike, and 100 miles of running. I was super proud, and I was like, 'This is the greatest thing ever,' and really it's rubbish because the next week you end up doing half of that, being absolutely fatigued and getting no quality. Which is why

creating a more scientific approach made sense."

Now you're the first person ever to win a gold medal in the Olympics and to win a gold medal at the IRONMAN World Championship. Which was more impactful?

"In terms of public perception and the hype around it, Kona was massive; it was way bigger. I went from being one of the guys out there to being a fairly big deal."

Did it surprise you that it was bigger than the Olympics?

"Yeah, it did, it did very much. It's like Kona and triathlon seem synonymous."

In 2016, you come back to Hawai`i to defend your title. You and Sebastian Kienle are together during the early part of the run and there's a little chatting going on. What were you guys talking about?

"I was just trying to slow him down. I was on the ropes, I was hurting. He was asking me about Lionel Sanders and how far back he was, and I'm like, 'Dude, there's like 20 other guys, what about their splits?' Anything to break his focus and his iron will just a little. That being said, we are good mates."

When I chatted with you afterwards you were

like, **"I didn't know if I was going to be able to go another mile."**

"It was one of those days when you take a whole year, and you focus your entire season on one day, and you just don't feel great. You know you've got the strength, you know you've done the miles, you know you've done the training, but... I was just playing defense. When Luke McKenzie went up the road, I gave everything I had – and a little bit more – just to try and bridge the gap. It was a very, very tough day, which of course in hindsight makes it very rewarding."

One other thing. At Kona people always talk about the heat, and the wind, and all the rest of it. I always feel that what makes that race special is the competition, because it's so deep.

"Yeah, definitely. You see guys, not a lot, but you always see a handful of guys who lose that race at the race briefing and it's a fierce room to be in, with some of the fittest people in the world, so you have a bit of a stare down. That's what a World Championship is all about – having the best guys face off and, yeah, hopefully having a great race."

◄ Let the celebrations begin! Jan Frodeno crossing the line at the end of a very tough, but very rewarding, day in 2016.

PATRICK LANGE

Date of Birth: August 25, 1986
Nationality: ▮▮▮▮▮

Honours:
2016 – IRONMAN World Championship, third place
2017 – IRONMAN World Championship, first place
    IRONMAN World Championship course record,
    8:01:40

BIOGRAPHY
After competing in IRONMAN 70.3 events for a number of years, Patrick Lange decided to quit his job as a physiotherapist and train full-time. His risk immediately paid off, winning IRONMAN Texas on his first full-distance start, before placing third on his first appearance at the IRONMAN World Championship, breaking the run course record in the process.

His 2017 season was marred by difficult long-term injury, but nonetheless Lange made it to the start line at the IRONMAN World Championship and out-performed everyone's expectations. He crossed the line in first place, ensuring his name went down among the IRONMAN legends by finishing in a course-record time of 8:01:40. In a mark of what embodies the IRONMAN spirit, he interrupted his celebrations to apologize to the previous record-holder, Craig Alexander.

Patrick Lange's interview with Bob Babbitt shortly after winning the 2017 IRONMAN World Championship

BB: You came to Kona for the first time in 2016 and came off the bike in twenty-third, after a penalty. You run 2:39:45 and break the run course record, taking third place. How did getting third change your life?
PL: "I was coming from almost no sponsorships at the end of 2015 to a whole new level. At the end of 2015, I was almost at the point of ending my career. That breakthrough performance in Hawai`i in 2016 opened up so many doors to help me get through the next year as a professional athlete. It changed my life completely."

There's a difference between having a great run to place and having a great run to win the race. You came off the bike in 2017 around 10 minutes behind Lionel Sanders and he ran a 2:51 marathon. Buy you ran 2:39:59. Did you feel more pressure this time?
"No, I didn't feel more pressure because I think pressure's always something that is generated from the outside. I try to focus on myself, and I had a good talk with my coach, Faris Al-Sultan, before the race. He told me that I have to stay within myself and if I just execute my performance, then I'm always good for a top-five position. Even coming off of injury at the beginning of the race, I didn't put too much pressure on myself.

"I was not in perfect shape, so the plan going into the race was just to execute the best race I can. I believed in my race plan, even if the bike portion was really bad for me."

You mentioned the three months when you were dealing with injuries and setbacks. Talk a little bit about that. You had something wrong, but you didn't know what it was.
"It all started in January at my first training camp in South Africa. I had so many new possibilities, and I was really motivated, so I really pushed hard in training. I tried some new bike shoes and new pedals to gain that little extra advantage. But, honestly, I forgot a little bit about recovery by doing that, and I was out of balance. I think when you are at the top level and if you are just a tiny little bit out of balance then things can change so quickly. I had a little pain in my foot, and I thought, 'Oh, that's not a big deal, just keep training'. I wanted to prove that the 2016 race was not just a fluke; that I could do even better than third place.

"In Germany, we have so many great athletes, and the media is really fast in saying, 'Yeah, this was just his first good IRONMAN race in Hawai`i.' I wanted to prove them wrong. I was focused and I was really pushing. And I think I was overdoing it a little bit. At the end of February, I needed time off. I was too tired to even get in the pool.

"We couldn't really find out what was wrong. We did an MRI and saw that there was a bone bruise in my foot, but the fatigue was the real problem. I was visiting a friend for a birthday party, and during lunchtime I was sleeping with my face on the table.

"It took eight doctor's visits to find the right guy who could really help me. He figured out that I had some sort of quicksilver and lead poisoning, which I didn't know was even possible."
What did he feel the lead poisoning was from?
"I had some really old fillings in my teeth. It was

like a quicksilver-lead combination. Due to the stress, I was grinding my teeth during the night. I also found out that when I was in the training camp, because I was so short on time, I would just grab some pasta with tomato sauce and add tuna. I'd eat three, four cans of tuna a day, and the cans are aluminum and the tuna is overloaded with lead, and all that other heavy metal stuff...

"It was just too much to handle for my body. So the doctor helped me to get rid of it. After two or three treatments, I was able to run again."

When were you able to get back to training?
"It was eight weeks before IRONMAN Frankfurt. Looking back on the performance in Frankfurt, I went 7:52 with a 2:49 marathon, but the second part of the marathon I was walking more than running. I was not happy with my performance right after the race, but when I look back now, I'm really happy to get that result out of just eight weeks of training."

You took third at Kona in 2016. I remember you saying that when you got off the plane you ended up on one of the big TV shows in Germany. That was for coming third. This time you won the race. What happened when you got home?
"It was crazy. I didn't count them, but I think there were at least 100 people at the airport waiting for me. It was very emotional."

You also broke Craig Alexander's course record.
"The race is only over when you cross the finish line. Even when I passed Lionel Sanders to go into the lead, I never stopped pushing. I saw the clock on the lead car and it read 7:40. I'm not good at math, but that was a calculation that I could do. But I put the thought away and focused again on just running. I didn't even think about breaking a record. When I came across the line, [race announcer] Mike Reilly said it was a new course record. It was just too much to handle for me, as an emotional person."

Think back to before you won IRONMAN North American Championship Texas, when you weren't sure if you could make it as a professional triathlete. If someone had told you back then, "Stay patient, you're going to win IRONMAN Texas, and then you're going to get third at Kona. And then the following year, you're going to win the IRONMAN World Championship," what would you have said?
"That person would have had to reach deep down in my soul, you know what I mean? Deep, deep down inside of me I knew that I was

capable of bigger things. If I didn't believe that I had the strength to at least win an IRONMAN race, I'm not saying winning Kona, but at least be good at it, I wouldn't be here. I definitely would have called him a little bit crazy. But on the other hand, I was always dreaming of it. We always say that if you can dream it, you can do it. I think that's true."

▼ Patrick Lange has time to start the celebrations with the crowd before crossing the finish line in 2017.

DANIELA RYF

Date of Birth: May 29, 1987
Nationality:

Honours:
2014 – IRONMAN World Championship, second place
IRONMAN 70.3 World Championship, first place
2015 – IRONMAN World Championship, first place
IRONMAN 70.3 World Championship, first place
2016 – IRONMAN World Championship, first place
2017 – IRONMAN World Championship, first place
IRONMAN 70.3 World Championship, first place

BIOGRAPHY
Daniela Ryf became a full-time triathlete in 2007, a year before making her Olympic debut in China, where she placed seventh. After another appearance in 2012,

Daniela decided to make a change – first to her coach, switching to Australian Brett Sutton, and then to her discipline, stepping up to the distance of IRONMAN races. This proved to be a good move in 2014 as she beat Brit Jodie Swallow by over two minutes at the IRONMAN 70.3 World Championship in Quebec before settling for silver after being overtaken late on by a fast-finishing Mirinda Carfrae in the IRONMAN World Championship.

Daniela proved that this performance was not a one-off the following year when she defended her IRONMAN 70.3 World Championship title by an awesome 11 minutes 33 seconds, and went even better in the IRONMAN World Championship to claim her first gold, outpacing Rachel Joyce by more than 13 minutes. Her year was completed when she was named Swiss Sports Personality of the Year. Since then, Daniela is unbeatable in the IRONMAN World Championship.

Daniela Ryf's interview with Bob Babbitt after winning her third IRONMAN World Championship

BB: In the 2017 IRONMAN World Championship, you see Lucy Charles and Lauren Brandon go off the front and obviously they're trying to get you out of your comfort zone. They're trying to put pressure on you to go harder on the bike than maybe you want to. What were you thinking?
DR: "Well, they succeeded with that, they definitely put the pressure on me. And, yeah, they challenged me all day. It was a new situation for me and they did have a fantastic swim and they are strong bikers too. It was hard for me. I didn't expect to struggle that much to catch up. I assumed they were just riding fast, and I wasn't riding fast enough to be able to catch them. When you have a plan and things don't go like the plan, you have to restructure and rethink, and that's what I tried to do. It put me out of my comfort zone, and I had to get a new plan to figure out how I could actually turn this race around. Because at 100 miles I was still five minutes back, and that was a challenge. It was a challenging race.
That was the moment: 87 miles into the bike ride, with 25 miles left, and you went from five minutes back to the lead. At that point you needed to take a chance, because you didn't want to get off the bike five minutes back.
"I was thinking, Okay, if I want to win this race I have to do something now. I have to switch off

my computer and start it new, and just give it all I have."
So ignore the power and all the rest of that stuff and just go?
"I decided to just think of it as a 25-mile time trial without any run left, and that's what I did. I gave it all I had and I risked maybe not being able to run at all. I rode for my life, to be honest. I was pushing as hard I ever had, and my feet were burning, and everything hurt. But it was worth the effort and I think mentally it changed the whole game.
"Because when you start to catch up you actually…"
You feel better?
"You feel better. When you're in pain, it's easier to handle if you realize you're actually making up time, and I think that was the turning point in the race, and that's probably where I won the race."
You felt it was imperative that you get into the transition first. Why?
"It was not so much about getting into transition first, but I knew that I also had girls behind me that were good runners.
"I had two girls five minutes in front of me, and I knew that position was not going to give me a very good opportunity for a win if I started to run that far back. That's why I wanted to change something, and yeah, I didn't plan to get off the bike first; I just wanted to make up time so I didn't have to make up five minutes in the run. I ended up catching them and being able to run out of transition

in first place, which really surprised me. I didn't expect that, and that was probably why I was so excited and confident, feeling that I could actually win the race. On the bike I did have a few moments where I wasn't sure how it was going to end, this race, and it was a rollercoaster of emotions. I think that's what racing is about. You have to dig deep in certain moments and just try to think positive.

"It ended up being a fantastic race, and a fantastic run, and I'm just very, very happy about how the race unfolded."

Did your legs feel OK after going that hard in the last part of the bike?

"When I jumped off the bike, my legs didn't feel okay. It was very painful. It took me a little time to get into it, but I was strong. Because I was leading, I could build the pressure on the girls, which is a nicer situation than when you have the pressure from the others. I'm really happy with my run. It hurt a lot, it was not an easy day, and I had to really fight hard for the win."

When you're coming down Ali'i Drive, and you're going to win the IRONMAN World Championship for the third time, you're joining a very select group in terms of winning three in a row... any thoughts in terms of your legacy? While you're in the midst of your career it's always difficult to talk about a legacy, that's usually something you talk about when you're done. But do you get a sense that you're building a pretty amazing reputation and a legacy here?

"To be honest, I haven't really realized that. It was so special just to be able to win the World Championship again. That, for me, was such a big thing. And to win the 2017 race was even more special because it was not..."

It wasn't easy?

"It didn't feel easy at all. And then of course it's amazing to be able to do it three times in a row. If you asked me that in 2013, I wouldn't have dared to dream about that. I'm just so happy with the race and that everything came out good in the end."

▲ Daniela Ryf looks composed after completing her hat trick of victories at the IRONMAN World Championship in 2017.

IRONMAN
STATS

The IRONMAN® World Championship and – since 2006 – the IRONMAN 70.3® World Championship annually play host to the world's greatest endurance athletes. This chapter details the men and women who have triumphed on each occasion, as well as those who, by breaking the Championship records, have gone one step further than all of those who have come before them.

◀ Patrick Lange, who broke the IRONMAN World Championship course record in 2017.

IRONMAN® WORLD CHAMPIONSHIP RESULTS

1978	Swim	Bike	Run	Total
Male: 1 – Gordon Haller	1:20:40	6:56:00	3:30:00	11:46:40
2 – John Dunbar	1:00:15	7:04:00	4:03:00	12:20:27
3 – Dave Orlowski	1:09:15	7:51:00	4:59:00	13:59:13
1979				
Male: 1 – Tom Warren	1:06:15	6:19:00	3:51:00	11:15:56
2 – John Dunbar	1:09:55	6:51:00	4:03:00	12:03:56
3 – Ian Emberson	1:02:35	6:53:00	4:28:00	12:23:30
Female: 1 – Lyn Lemaire	1:16:20	6:30:00	5:10:00	12:55:38
1980				
Male: 1 – Dave Scott	51:00	5:03:00	3:30:33	9:24:33
2 – Chuck Neumann	1:02:00	5:38:00	3:44:41	10:24:41
3 – John Howard	1:51:00	4:28:00	4:13:36	10:32:36
Female: 1 – Robin Beck	1:20:00	6:05:00	3:56:24	11:21:24
2 – Eve Anderson	1:30:00	7:48:00	6:22:59	15:40:59
1981				
Male: 1 – John Howard	1:11:12	5:03:29	3:23:48	9:38:29
2 – Tom Warren	59:40	5:37:09	3:27:49	10:04:38
3 – Scott Tinley	1:05:34	5:47:52	3:19:21	10:12:47
Female: 1 – Linda Sweeney	1:02:07	6:53:28	4:04:57	12:00:32
2 – Sally Edwards	1:28:30	6:58:36	4:10:19	12:37:25
3 – Lyn Brooks	1:20:07	7:13:11	4:08:57	12:42:15
1982 (February)				
Male: 1 – Scott Tinley	1:10:45	5:05:11	3:03:45	9:19:41
2 – Dave Scott	58:39	5:17:16	3:21:02	9:36:57
3 – Jeff Tinley	1:13:02	5:27:45	3:12:29	9:53:16
Female: 1 – Kathleen McCartney	1:32:00	5:51:12	3:46:28	11:09:40
2 – Julie Moss	1:11:00	5:53:39	4:05:30	11:10:09
3= – Lyn Brooks	1:19:30	6:38:02	3:53:29	11:51:00
3= - Sally Edwards	1:36:30	6:30:06	3:44:24	11:51:00
1982 (October)				
Male: 1 – Dave Scott	50:52	5:10:16	3:07:15	9:08:23
2 – Scott Tinley	1:00:58	5:18:09	3:09:21	9:28:28
3 – Jeff Tinley	58:05	5:21:05	3:17:43	9:36:53
Female: 1 – Julie Leach	1:04:57	5:50:36	3:58:35	10:54:08
2 – Jo Ann Dahlkoetter	1:14:04	6:02:29	3:41:48	10:58:21
3 – Sally Edwards	1:15:38	6:19:27	3:27:55	11:03:00
1983				
Male: 1 – Dave Scott	50:52	5:10:46	3:04:16	9:05:57
2 – Scott Tinley	57:24	5:03:58	3:05:08	9:06:30
3 – Mark Allen	52:08	5:13:32	3:15:26	9:21:06
Female: 1 – Sylviane Puntous	1:00:28	6:20:40	3:22:28	10:43:36
2 – Patricia Puntous	1:00:31	6:26:12	3:22:33	10:49:17
3 – Eva Ueltzen	1:02:48	6:05:13	3:53:48	11:01:49

1984				
Male: 1 – Dave Scott	50:21	5:10:59	2:53:00	8:54:20
2 – Scott Tinley	55:54	5:18:52	3:03:57	9:18:45
3 – Grant Boswell	53:07	5:15:04	3:15:44	9:23:55
Female: 1 – Sylviane Puntous	1:00:45	5:50:36	3:33:51	10:25:13
2 – Patricia Puntous	1:00:51	5:50:31	3:36:05	10:27:28
3 – Julie Olson	1:00:33	5:37:43	3:59:54	10:38:10
1985				
Male: 1 – Scott Tinley	55:13	4:54:07	3:01:33	8:50:54
2 – Christopher Hinshaw	49:53	4:57:50	3:28:56	9:16:40
3 – Carl Kupferschmid	1:11:47	5:10:35	3:04:09	9:26:32
Female: 1 – Joanne Ernst	1:01:42	5:39:13	3:44:26	10:25:22
2 – Elizabeth Bulman	1:01:11	6:01:16	3:24:27	10:26:55
3 – Paula Newby- Fraser	59:38	5:54:26	3:36:59	10:31:04
1986				
Male: 1 – Dave Scott	50:53	4:48:32	2:49:11	8:28:37
2 – Mark Allen	51:00	4:49:29	2:55:34	8:36:04
3 – Scott Tinley	53:06	4:57:18	3:10:11	9:00:37
Female: 1 – Paula Newby- Fraser	57:03	5:32:05	3:20:05	9:49:14
2 – Sylviane Puntous	56:24	5:34:57	3:21:51	9:53:13
3 – Joanne Ernst	57:36	5:26:09	3:36:21	10:00:07
1987				
Male: 1 – Dave Scott	50:57	4:53:48	2:49:26	8:34:13
2 – Mark Allen	51:00	4:53:47	3:00:31	8:45:19
3 – Greg Stewart	1:03:16	5:00:00	2:55:36	8:58:53
Female: 1 – Erin Baker	57:42	5:26:34	3:11:08	9:35:25
2 – Sylviane Puntous	57:50	5:29:43	3:08:23	9:36:57
3 – Paula Newby- Fraser	58:03	5:22:15	3:20:18	9:40:37
1988				
Male: 1 – Scott Molina	51:28	4:36:50	3:02:42	8:31:00
2 – Michael Pigg	51:20	4:37:44	3:04:06	8:33:11
3 – Ken Glah	51:29	4:40:20	3:06:47	8:38:37
Female: 1 – Paula Newby- Fraser	56:38	4:57:13	3:07:09	9:01:01
2 – Erin Baker	55:39	5:04:02	3:12:32	9:12:14
3 – Kirsten Hannsen	1:00:23	5:12:46	3:24:15	9:37:25
1989				
Male: 1 – Mark Allen	51:17	4:37:52	2:40:04	8:09:15
2 – Dave Scott	51:16	4:37:53	2:41:03	8:10:13
3 – Greg Welch	51:39	4:43:43	2:56:53	8:32:16
Female: 1 – Paula Newby-Fraser	54:19	5:01:00	3:05:37	9:00:56
2 – Sylviane Puntous	56:33	5:09:28	3:15:53	9:21:55
3 – Kirsten Hanssen	53:52	5:05:17	3:25:22	9:24:31

1990

Male: 1 – Mark Allen	51:43	4:43:45	2:52:48	8:28:17
2 – Scott Tinley	52:36	4:51:33	2:53:30	8:37:40
3 – Pauli Kiuru	52:48	4:51:32	2:55:04	8:39:24
Female: 1 – Erin Baker	56:37	5:12:52	3:04:13	9:13:42
2 – Paula Newby-Fraser	57:05	5:14:45	3:08:10	9:20:01
3 – Terri Schneider	1:01:56	5:32:12	3:26:25	10:00:34

1991

Male: 1 – Mark Allen	50:14	4:46:07	2:42:09	8:18:32
2 – Greg Welch	51:02	4:45:21	2:48:10	8:24:34
3 – Jeff Devlin	54:12	4:43:11	2:50:31	8:27:55
Female: 1 – Paula Newby-Fraser	54:59	5:05:47	3:07:05	9:07:52
2 – Erin Baker	56:32	5:08:47	3:18:18	9:23:37
3 – Sarah Coope	1:02:34	5:19:09	3:11:36	9:33:20

1992

Male: 1 – Mark Allen	51:27	4:35:23	2:42:18	8:09:08
2 – Cristian Bustos	52:35	4:34:16	2:49:38	8:16:29
3 – Pauli Kiuru	51:18	4:36:26	2:49:45	8:17:29
Female: 1 – Paula Newby-Fraser	53:30	4:56:34	3:05:24	8:55:28
2 – Julie Anne White	1:02:07	5:02:32	3:17:01	9:21:40
3 – Thea Sybesma	1:00:40	5:08:14	3:18:03	9:26:57

1993

Male: 1 – Mark Allen	50:40	4:29:00	2:48:05	8:07:45
2 – Pauli Kiuru	51:05	4:28:06	2:55:16	8:14:27
3 – Wolfgang Dittrich	48:30	4:30:29	3:01:14	8:20:13
Female: 1 – Paula Newby-Fraser	53:29	4:48:30	3:16:24	8:58:23
2 – Erin Baker	58:36	4:50:16	3:19:12	9:08:04
3 – Susan Latshaw	56:05	4:57:49	3:26:46	9:20:40

1994

Male: 1 – Greg Welch	50:22	4:41:07	2:48:58	8:20:27
2 – Dave Scott	51:48	4:39:16	2:53:28	8:24:32
3 – Jeff Devlin	58:49	4:34:06	2:59:01	8:31:56
Female: 1 – Paula Newby-Fraser	54:19	5:02:25	3:23:30	9:20:14
2 – Karen Smyers	58:22	5:10:55	3:18:51	9:28:08
3 – Fernanda Keller	1:05:05	5:15:39	3:22:46	9:43:30

1995

Male: 1 – Mark Allen	51:50	4:46:35	2:42:09	8:20:34
2 – Thomas Hellriegel	55:17	4:29:37	2:58:05	8:22:59
3 – Rainer Muller-Horner	52:12	4:45:54	2:47:17	8:25:23
Female: 1 – Karen Smyers	53:37	5:17:49	3:05:20	9:16:46
2 – Isabelle Mouthon	55:15	5:17:51	3:12:07	9:25:13
3 – Fernanda Keller	1:02:08	5:17:53	3:17:47	9:37:48

1996

Male: 1 – Luc Van Lierde	51:36	4:30:44	2:41:48	8:04:08
2 – Thomas Hellriegel	54:22	4:30:44	2:46:55	8:06:07
3 – Greg Welch	51:23	4:35:43	2:51:51	8:18:57
Female: 1 – Paula Newby-Fraser	55:30	5:01:34	3:09:45	9:06:49
2 – Natascha Badmann	1:00:41	4:53:47	3:16:51	9:11:19
3 – Karen Smyers	54:11	5:02:33	3:22:29	9:19:13

1997

Male: 1 – Thomas Hellriegel	53:08	4:47:57	2:51:56	8:33:01
2 – Jurgen Zack	52:12	4:45:33	3:01:33	8:39:18
3 – Lothar Leder	52:22	4:58:53	2:49:15	8:40:30
Female: 1 – Heather Fuhr	1:01:47	5:23:11	3:06:45	9:31:43
2 – Lori Bowden	1:04:43	5:15:26	3:21:33	9:41:42
3 – Fernanda Keller	57:27	5:26:51	3:25:44	9:50:02

1998

Male: 1 – Peter Reid	52:04	4:42:23	2:47:31	8:24:20
2 – Luc Van Lierde	48:48	4:52:45	2:47:58	8:31:57
3 – Lothar Leder	50:43	4:55:20	2:44:58	8:32:57
Female: 1 – Natascha Badmann	56:02	5:10:00	3:14:50	9:24:16
2 – Lori Bowden	1:01:43	5:15:54	3:07:03	9:27:19
3 – Fernanda Keller	55:43	5:18:14	3:12:17	9:28:29

1999

Male: 1 – Luc Van Lierde	50:38	4:41:26	2:42:26	8:17:17
2 – Peter Reid	50:46	4:41:39	2:47:56	8:22:54
3 – Tim DeBoom	48:51	4:42:58	2:51:23	8:25:42
Female: 1 – Lori Bowden	1:02:23	5:08:30	2:59:16	9:13:02
2 – Karen Smyers	53:03	5:15:01	3:09:33	9:20:40
3 – Fernanda Keller	56:04	5:16:33	3:09:30	9:24:30

2000

Male: 1 – Peter Reid	51:45	4:39:32	2:48:10	8:21:00
2 – Tim DeBoom	50:33	4:40:30	2:49:59	8:23:09
3 – Normann Stadler	52:51	4:35:14	2:56:00	8:26:44
Female: 1 – Natascha Badmann	58:04	5:06:42	3:19:02	9:26:16
2 – Lori Bowden	1:00:26	5:21:33	3:04:19	9:29:04
3 – Fernanda Keller	56:37	5:22:11	3:10:43	9:31:28

2001

Male: 1 – Tim DeBoom	52:01	4:48:17	2:45:54	8:31:18
2 – Cameron Brown	52:16	4:53:29	2:58:05	8:46:10
3 – Thomas Hellriegel	55:35	4:47:42	3:01:25	8:47:40
Female: 1 – Natascha Badmann	59:55	5:16:07	3:09:33	9:28:37
2 – Lori Bowden	1:01:04	5:25:55	3:03:09	9:32:59
3 – Nina Kraft	54:09	5:29:30	3:14:18	9:41:01

2002

Male: 1 – Tim DeBoom	52:02	4:45:21	2:50:22	8:29:56
2 – Peter Reid	53:20	4:44:15	2:53:48	8:33:06
3 – Cameron Brown	52:13	4:45:15	2:56:06	8:35:34
Female: 1 – Natascha Badmann	59:40	4:52:26	3:12:58	9:07:54
2 – Nina Kraft	53:27	5:06:15	3:12:03	9:14:24
3 – Lori Bowden	59:52	5:08:02	3:09:32	9:22:27

2003

Male: 1 – Peter Reid	50:36	4:40:04	2:47:38	8:22:35
2 – Rutger Beke	52:28	4:37:59	2:54:12	8:28:27
3 – Cameron Brown	50:38	4:39:57	2:57:29	8:32:02
Female: 1 – Lori Bowden	56:51	5:09:00	3:02:10	9:11:55
2 – Natascha Badmann	58:43	5:00:02	3:13:45	9:17:08
3 – Nina Kraft	51:45	5:07:34	3:11:18	9:17:16

2004

Male: 1 – Normann Stadler	54:27	4:37:58	2:57:52	8:33:29
2 – Peter Reid	53:12	5:01:38	2:46:09	8:43:40
3 – Faris Al-Sultan	50:39	4:55:44	2:54:51	8:45:14
Female: 1 – Natascha Badmann	1:01:3	5:31:37	3:11:45	9:50:04
2 – Heather Fuhr	1:01:18	5:44:12	3:06:04	9:56:19
3 – Kate Major	1:01:05	5:38:51	3:17:38	10:01:56

2005

Male: 1 – Faris Al-Sultan	49:54	4:25:22	2:54:51	8:14:17
2 – Cameron Brown	52:23	4:33:06	2:50:13	8:19:36
3 – Peter Reid	52:23	4:27:49	2:55:59	8:20:04
Female: 1 – Natascha Badmann	1:02:30	4:51:58	3:06:24	9:09:30
2 – Michellie Jones	54:55	4:54:11	3:18:13	9:11:51
3 – Kate Major	1:00:07	5:06:10	3:012:19	9:12:39

2006

Male: 1 – Normann Stadler	54:05	4:18:23	2:55:02	8:11:56
2 – Chris McCormack	53:51	4:29:23	2:46:01	8:13:07
3 – Faris Al-Sultan	53:36	4:29:37	2:50:44	8:19:04
Female: 1 – Michellie Jones	54:29	5:06:09	3:13:08	9:18:31
2 – Desiree Ficker	1:01:46	5:05:06	3:11:49	9:24:02
3 – Lisa Bentley	1:01:31	5:10:31	3:08:53	9:25:18

2007

Male: 1 – Chris McCormack	51:48	4:37:31	2:42:02	8:15:34
2 – Craig Alexander	51:40	4:38:11	2:45:13	8:19:04
3 – Torbjorn Sindballe	53:25	4:25:26	2:57:25	8:21:30
Female: 1 – Chrissie Wellington	58:09	5:06:15	2:59:57	9:08:45
2 – Samantha McGlone	58:07	5:10:31	3:00:51	9:14:04
3 – Kate Major	58:08	5:10:16	3:06:35	9:19:13

2008

Male: 1 – Craig Alexander	51:43	4:37:19	2:45:00	8:17:45
2 – Eneko Llanos	51:39	4:33:26	2:51:48	8:20:50
3 – Rutger Beke	54:44	4:34:44	2:47:49	8:21:23
Female: 1 – Chrissie Wellington	56:20	5:08:15	2:57:44	9:06:23
2 – Yvonne van Vlerken	1:06:49	5:05:34	3:04:26	9:21:20
3 – Sandra Wallenhorst	1:03:21	5:14:56	2:58:35	9:22:52

2009

Male: 1 – Craig Alexander	50:57	4:37:33	2:48:05	8:20:21
2 – Chris Lieto	51:07	4:25:10	3:02:35	8:22:56
3 – Andreas Raelert	51:00	4:38:00	2:51:04	8:24:32
Female: 1 – Chrissie Wellington	54:31	4:52:06	3:03:05	8:54:02
2 – Mirinda Carfrae	58:45	5:14:17	2:56:51	9:13:59
3 – Virginia Berasategui	58:52	5:01:41	3:10:43	9:15:28

2010

Male: 1 – Chris McCormack	51:36	4:31:50	2:43:31	8:10:37
2 – Andreas Raelert	51:27	4:32:26	2:44:25	8:12:17
3 – Marino Vanhoenacker	51:33	4:31:00	2:46:45	8:13:14
Female: 1 – Mirinda Carfrae	55:53	5:04:59	2:53:32	8:58:36
2 – Caroline Steffen	55:57	4:59:22	3:05:47	9:06:00
3 – Julie Dibens	53:50	4:55:27	3:16:12	9:10:04

2011

Male: 1 – Craig Alexander	51:56	4:24:05	2:44:02	8:03:56
2 – Pete Jacobs	51:38	4:31:01	2:42:29	8:09:11
3 – Andreas Raelert	51:58	4:26:52	2:47:47	8:11:07
Female: 1 – Chrissie Wellington	1:01:0	4:56:53	2:52:41	8:55:08
2 – Mirinda Carfrae	57:17	5:04:16	2:52:09	8:57:57
3 – Leanda Cave	53:54	4:58:41	3:06:36	9:03:29

2012

Male: 1 – Pete Jacobs	51:28	4:35:15	2:48:05	8:18:37
2 – Andreas Raelert	55:17	4:36:34	2:47:23	8:23:40
3 – Frederik Van Lierde	51:36	4:35:25	2:52:49	8:24:09
Female: 1 – Leanda Cave	56:03	5:12:06	3:03:13	9:15:54
2 – Caroline Steffen	57:37	5:06:49	3:08:08	9:16:58
3 – Mirinda Carfrae	1:00:06	5:12:18	3:05:04	9:21:41

2013

Male: 1 – Frederik Van Lierde	51:02	4:25:35	2:51:18	8:12:29
2 – Luke McKenzie	51:17	4:22:25	2:57:20	8:15:19
3 – Sebastian Kienle	54:13	4:22:33	2:58:35	8:19:24
Female: 1 – Mirinda Carfrae	58:50	4:58:20	2:50:38	8:52:14
2 – Rachel Joyce	54:09	4:55:25	3:03:37	8:57:28
3 – Liz Blatchford	54:07	4:57:40	3:03:23	9:03:35

2014

Male: 1 – Sebastian Kienle	54:38	4:20:46	2:54:36	8:14:18
2 – Ben Hoffman	51:20	4:32:20	2:51:25	8:19:23
3 – Jan Frodeno	50:56	4:37:19	2:47:46	8:20:32
Female: 1 – Mirinda Carfrae	1:00:14	5:05:48	2:50:26	9:00:55
2 – Daniela Ryf	56:55	4:54:33	3:07:00	9:02:57
3 – Rachel Joyce	56:47	4:56:49	3:06:27	9:04:23

2015

Male: 1 – Jan Frodeno	50:50	4:27:27	2:52:21	8:14:40
2 – Andreas Raelert	52:24	4:30:52	2:50:02	8:17:43
3 – Tim O'Donnell	52:24	4:26:13	2:55:46	8:18:50
Female: 1 – Daniela Ryf	56:14	4:50:46	3:06:37	8:57:57
2 – Rachel Joyce	56:11	5:01:29	3:08:42	9:10:59
3 – Liz Blatchford	56:13	5:07:25	3:06:25	9:14:52

2016

Male: 1 – Jan Frodeno	48:02	4:29:00	2:45:34	8:06:30
2 – Sebastian Kienle	52:27	4:23:55	2:49:03	8:10:02
3 – Patrick Lange	48:57	4:37:49	2:39:45	8:11:14
Female: 1 – Daniela Ryf	52:50	4:52:26	2:56:51	8:46:46
2 – Mirinda Carfrae	56:44	5:10:54	2:58:20	9:10:30
3 – Heather Jackson	58:56	5:00:31	3:07:48	9:11:32

2017

Male: 1 – Patrick Lange	48:45	4:28:53	2:39:59	8:01:40
2 – Lionel Sanders	53:41	4:14:19	2:51:53	8:04:07
3 – David McNamee	48:40	4:28:55	2:45:30	8:07:11
Female: 1 – Daniela Ryf	53:10	4:53:10	3:00:02	8:50:47
2 – Lucy Charles	48:48	4:58:19	3:08:09	8:59:38
3 – Sarah Crowley	53:07	4:57:51	3:05:36	9:01:38

IRONMAN 70.3® WORLD CHAMPIONSHIP RESULTS

2006		Swim	Bike	Run	Total
Male: 1 – Craig Alexander		24:08	2:05:35	1:12:43	3:45:38
2 – Simon Lessing		24:05	2:05:27	1:14:11	3:47:28
3 – Richie Cunningham		24:02	2:05:39	1:16:20	3:49:19
Female: 1 – Samantha McGlone		27:29	2:21:33	1:20:22	4:12:59
2 – Lisa Bentley		27:49	2:21:04	1:21:33	4:14:32
3 – Mirinda Carfrae		27:33	2:21:11	1:24:00	4:16:46

2007					
Male: 1 – Andy Potts		22:57	2:04:29	1:11:33	3:42:33
2 – Oscar Galindez		25:07	2:00:28	1:13:02	3:42:37
3 – Andrew Johns		23:30	2:04:11	1:12:05	3:43:11
Female: 1 – Mirinda Carfrae		26:33	2:18:32	1:18:40	4:07:25
2 – Samantha McGlone		27:46	2:19:00	1:20:51	4:11:29
3 – Leanda Cave		25:16	2:17:12	1:25:55	4:12:29

2008					
Male: 1 – Terenzo Bozzone		22:17	2:01:29	1:12:57	3:40:10
2 – Andreas Raelert		22:22	2:03:27	1:10:54	3:40:42
3 – Richie Cunningham		22:29	2:02:08	1:10:54	3:41:47
Female: 1 – Joanna Zeiger		23:06	2:13:44	1:21:59	4:02:49
2 – Mary Beth Ellis		23:23	2:13:19	1:23:19	4:04:07
3 – Becky Lavelle		23:03	2:13:50	1:26:46	4:07:32

2009					
Male: 1 – Michael Raelert		21:58	1:59:35	1:09:06	3:34:04
2 – Daniel Fontana		21:55	1:59:30	1:12:00	3:36:44
3 – Matthew Reed		21:59	1:59:09	1:13:11	3:37:50
Female: 1 – Julie Dibens		23:48	2:07:15	1:24:37	3:59:33
2 – Mary Beth Ellis		24:05	2:10:58	1:24:42	4:03:49
3 – Magali Tisseyre		25:34	2:15:17	1:20:32	4:05:27

2010					
Male: 1 – Michael Raelert		24:16	2:03:58	1:09:57	3:41:19
2 – Filip Ospaly		23:19	2:04:56	1:11:24	3:42:56
3 – Timothy Odonnell		23:20	2:04:53	1:12:44	3:44:18
Female: 1 – Jodie Swallow		24:20	2:16:37	1:21:59	4:06:28
2 – Leanda Cave		25:56	2:18:57	1:23:15	4:12:34
3 – Magali Tisseyre		27:22	2:19:25	1:22:28	4:13:04

2011					
Male: 1 – Craig Alexander		24:45	2:14:47	1:11:51	3:54:48
2 – Chris Lieto		24:51	2:10:36	1:18:56	3:58:03
3 – Jeff Symonds		24:47	2:16:55	1:13:33	3:58:42
Female: 1 – Melissa Rollison		28:27	2:27:58	1:21:14	4:20:55
2 – Karin Thuerig		33:01	2:24:05	1:25:15	4:26:52
3 – Linsey Corbin		29:19	2:31:08	1:25:24	4:29:25

2012		Swim	Bike	Run	Total
Male: 1 – Sebastian Kienle		26:32	2:07:54	1:16:45	3:54:35
2 – Craig Alexander		23:54	2:13:23	1:14:58	3:55:36
3 – Bevan Docherty		23:51	2:13:41	1:15:35	3:56:25
Female: 1 – Leanda Cave		26:07	2:28:17	1:29:53	4:28:05
2 – Kelly Williamson		26:05	2:36:26	1:23:19	4:29:24
3 – Heather Jackson		28:54	2:27:45	1:32:13	4:32:32

2013					
Male: 1 – Sebastian Kienle		25:38	2:10:10	1:14:50	3:54:02
2 – Terenzo Bozzone		24:36	2:14:31	1:13:38	3:56:06
3 – Joe Gambles		24:48	2:14:06	1:14:29	3:56:55
Female: 1 – Melissa Hauschildt		29:19	2:25:08	1:21:37	4:20:07
2 – Heather Jackson		30:08	2:28:48	1:22:55	4:25:19
3 – Annabel Luxford		25:59	2:28:38	1:27:24	4:25:59

2014					
Male: 1 – Javier Gomez Noya		22:09	2:06:18	1:09:27	3:41:30
2 – Jan Frodeno		22:10	2:05:48	1:10:36	3:42:11
3 – Tim Don		22:41	2:05:18	1:12:44	3:44:38
Female: 1 – Daniela Ryf		24:04	2:16:46	1:24:30	4:09:19
2 – Jodie Ann Swallow		23:59	2:19:28	1:24:10	4:11:43
3 – Heather Wurtele		26:24	2:21:53	1:22:19	4:14:55

2015					
Male: 1 – Jan Frodeno		22:14	2:09:04	1:16:32	3:51:19
2 – Sebastian Kienle		24:04	2:09:54	1:15:22	3:52:48
3 – Javier Gomez Noya		22:12	2:13:38	1:15:35	3:55:05
Female: 1 – Daniela Ryf		23:46	2:21:10	1:22:51	4:11:34
2 – Heather Wurtele		26:33	2:27:39	1:24:56	4:23:07
3 – Anja Beranek		24:32	2:24:18	1:31:17	4:24:10

2016					
Male: 1 – Timothy Reed		22:53	2:06:12	1:11:03	3:44:14
2 – Sebastian Kienle		24:14	2:04:45	1:11:18	3:44:16
3 – Ruedi Wild		22:47	2:06:28	1:11:07	3:44:40
Female: 1 – Holly Lawrence		23:24	2:19:28	1:21:48	4:09:12
2 – Melissa Hauschildt		26:46	2:21:06	1:18:43	4:11:09
3 – Heather Wurtele		25:05	2:22:26	1:21:38	4:13:36

2017					
Male: 1 – Javier Gomez Noya		24:08	2:12:27	1:10:29	3:49:44
2 – Ben Kanute		24:03	2:08:10	1:16:23	3:51:06
3 – Tim Don		24:58	2:11:12	1:13:04	3:51:59
Female: 1 – Daniela Ryf		26:26	2:20:20	1:22:05	4:11:59
2 – Emma Pallant		27:53	2:28:00	1:19:48	4:18:36
3 – Laura Philipp		29:47	2:25:45	1:21:12	4:19:40

PROGRESSIVE IRONMAN WORLD CHAMPIONSHIP COURSE RECORDS

Overall Male Course Record

Gordon Haller	11:46:40 (1978)
Tom Warren	11:15:56 (1979)
Dave Scott	9:24:33 (1980)
Scott Tinley	9:19:41 (1982 – Feb)
Dave Scott	9:08:23 (1982 – Oct)
Dave Scott	9:05:57 (1983)
Dave Scott	8:54:20 (1984)
Scott Tinley	8:50:54 (1985)
Dave Scott	8:28:37 (1986)
Mark Allen	8:09:15 (1989)
Mark Allen	8:09:08 (1992)
Mark Allen	8:07:45 (1993)
Luc Van Lierde	8:04:08 (1996)
Craig Alexander	8:03:56 (2011)
Patrick Lange	8:01:40 (2017)

Overall Female Course Record

Lyn Lemaire	12:55:38 (1979)
Robin Beck	11:21:24 (1980)
Kathleen McCartney	11:09:40 (1982 – Feb)
Julie Leach	10:54:08 (1982 – Oct)
Sylviane Puntous	10:43:36 (1983)
Sylviane Puntous	10:25:13 (1984)
Paula Newby- Fraser	9:49:14 (1986)
Erin Baker	9:35:25 (1987)
Paula Newby- Fraser	9:01:01 (1988)
Paula Newby-Fraser	9:00:56 (1989)
Paula Newby-Fraser	8:55:28 (1992)
Chrissie Wellington	8:54:02 (2009)
Mirinda Carfrae	8:52:14 (2013)
Daniela Ryf	8:46:46 (2016)

Male Swim Course Record

Archie Hapai	57:35 (1978)
Dave Scott	51:00 (1980)
Chris Hinshaw	50:34 (1983)
Djan Madruga	47:48 (1984)
Bradford Hinshaw	47:39 (1986)
Lars Jorgensen	46:44 (1995)
Lars Jorgensen	46:41 (1998)

Female Swim Course Record

Lyn Lemaire	1:16:20 (1979)
Shawn Wilson	1:01:18 (1981)
Jann Girard	53:35 (1983)
Jennifer Hinshaw	50:31 (1984)
Wendy Ingraham	49:52 (1997)
Wendy Ingraham	49:11 (1998)
Jodi Jackson	48:43 (1999)

Male Bike Course Record

Gordon Haller	6:56:00 (1978)
Tom Warren	6:19:00 (1979)
John Howard	4:28:00 (1980)
Jurgen Zack	4:27:42 (1993)
Thomas Hellriegel	4:24:50 (1996)
Torbjorn Sindballe	4:21:36 (2005)
Normann Stadler	4:18:23 (2006)
Cameron Wurf	4:12:54 (2017)

Female Bike Course Record

Lyn Lemaire	6:30:00 (1979)
Robin Beck	6:05:00 (1980)
Kathleen McCartney	5:51:12 (1982)
Julie Olson	5:37:43 (1984)
Joanne Ernst	5:26:09 (1986)
Paula Newby-Fraser	5:22:15 (1987)
Paula Newby-Fraser	4:57:13 (1988)
Paula Newby-Fraser	4:56:34 (1992)
Paula Newby-Fraser	4:48:30 (1993)
Karin Theurig	4:48:22 (2010)
Karin Theurig	4:44:19 (2011)

Male Run Course Records

Gordon Haller	3:30:00 (1978)
Gordon Haller	3:27:15 (1980)
Joe Kasbohm	2:59:48 (1981)
Dave Scott	2:53:00 (1984)
Dave Scott	2:49:11 (1986)
Mark Allen	2:40:04 (1989)
Patrick Lange	2:39:45 (2016)

Female Run Course Record

Lyn Lemaire	5:10:00 (1979)
Robin Beck	3:56:24 (1980)
Sally Edwards	3:44:24 (1982)
Sylviane Puntuous	3:22:28 (1983)
Beth Nelson	3:17:49 (1986)
Sylviane Puntuous	3:09:23 (1987)
Paula Newby-Fraser	3:07:09 (1988)
Paula Newby-Fraser	3:05:37 (1989)
Erin Baker	3:04:13 (1990)
Heather Fuhr	3:04:02 (1998)
Lori Bowden	2:59:16 (1999)
Chrissie Wellington	2:57:44 (2008)
Mirinda Carfrae	2:56:51 (2009)
Mirinda Carfrae	2:53:32 (2010)
Mirinda Carfrae	2:52:09 (2011)

PROGRESSIVE IRONMAN 70.3 WORLD CHAMPIONSHIP COURSE RECORDS

Overall Male Championship Record

Craig Alexander	3:45:38 (2006)
Andy Potts	3:42:33 (2007)
Terenzo Bozzone	3:40:10 (2008)
Michael Raelert	3:34:04 (2009)

Overall Female Championship Record

Samantha McGlone	4:12:59 (2006)
Mirinda Carfrae	4:07:25 (2007)
Joanna Zeiger	4:02:49 (2008)
Julie Dibens	3:59:33 (2009)

Male Swim Championship Record

Pete Jacobs	23:55 (2006)
David Kahn	22:30 (2007)
John Flanagan	20:55 (2008)

Female Swim Championship Record

Leanda Cave	25:13 (2006)
Julie Dibens	24:45 (2007)
Becky Lavelle	23:03 (2008)
Lauren Brandon	22:54 (2016)

Male Bike Championship Record

Chris Lieto	2:02:10 (2006)
Bjorn Andersson	1:59:38 (2007)
Andrew Starykowicz	1:59:49 (2009)

Female Bike Championship Record

Sara Megan Quinty	2:15:16 (2006)
Michele Wolfson	2:11:51 (2007)
Julie Dibens	2:07:15 (2009)

Male Run Championship Records

Craig Alexander	1:12:43 (2006)
Andy Potts	1:11:33 (2007)
Andreas Raelert	1:10:53 (2008)
Michael Raelert	1:09:05 (2009)

Female Run Championship Record

Samantha McGlone	1:20:22 (2006)
Mirinda Carfrae	1:18:41 (2007)

IRONMAN Hall of Fame

1993 – Dave Scott
1994 – Julie Moss
1995 – Scott Tinley
1996 – Paula Newby-Fraser
1997 – Mark Allen
1998 – John and Judy Collins
1999 – Valerie Silk
2000 – Tom Warren
2001 – Dr. Bob Laird
2002 – Bob Babbitt
2003 – Gordon Haller / John MacLean /
        Lyn Lemaire
2004 – Greg Welch
2005 – Jim MacLaren
2008 – Rick and Dick Hoyt
2011 – Mike Reilly
2012 – Graham Fraser
2013 – Peter Henning
2014 – Georg Hochegger / Stefan Petschnig /
        Helge Lorenz
2015 – Heather Fuhr / Lori Bowden
2016 – Peter Reid / Lew Friedland
2017 – Chrissie Wellington
2018 – Erin Baker / Scott Molina / Ken Baggs /
        Rocky Campbell

▶ Breaking the finish-line tape in 1992, Paula Newby-Fraser set a course record that stayed undefeated for an incredible 17 years.

Athletes dive into the 2015 IRONMAN European Championship in Frankfurt, where 15,000 spectators come each year to cheer them on.

 GLOSSARY

ALS: amyotrophic lateral sclerosis – a motor neuron disease also known as Lou Gehrig's disease. It causes the death of neurons controlling voluntary muscles and makes muscle use steadily more difficult.

Build swim: A swim in which the athlete increases their speed throughout each interval of the swim, from slow to fast.

CD: The cool down portion of a training session. This should be performed at an easy level of effort.

CGI: Competitor Group Holding, the San Diego-based company, bought by the Dalian Wanda Group in 2017, that ran a variety of endurance sport and triathlon events, including the Rock 'n' Roll marathon series.

CV: A bike ride in which the athlete utilizes cadence variance to improve training performance. During cadence variance the athlete alternates between a slow, medium and fast cadence.

Desc swim: A swim in which each interval is swum at a faster pace than the last.

DNF: Did Not Finish – the notation used when an athlete does not complete an IRONMAN triathlon.

Env run: An envelope run is a mindfulness exercise, in which an athlete focuses on running faster by using an improved technique, not increased effort.

EPO: Erythropoietin is a peptide hormone that is produced naturally by the human body. EPO is released from the kidneys and acts on the bone marrow to stimulate red blood cell production. EPO use increases athletic ability, for endurance athletes in particular, and its use in sport is banned by the World Anti-Doping Agency.

GPS: The Global Positioning System is a satellite-based radio-navigation system that provides geo-location information. Its use in sporting equipment allows athletes to track performance data far more accurately than previously.

HC: Handcycle – the IRONMAN Handcycle division is open to athletes who are paraplegic, quadriplegic or double above-the-knee amputees, and race using a hand cranked cycle on the bike, and a racing chair for the run.

ITU: The International Triathlon Union is the international governing body for various multi-sport disciplines, including triathlon.

MND: *See ALS*

MRI: Magnetic Resonance Imaging is a medical imaging technique used in radiology to form pictures of the anatomy and the physiological processes of the body in both health and disease.

NFL: National Football League – the U.S. professional American football league.

PB: A personal best is the best time achieved by an athlete in any particular sport or event.

PC: Physically Challenged – participation in the IRONMAN PC Open Division is available to athletes with a medically verified visual impairment or a medically verified physical or neurological impairment that substantially limits one or more major life activities.

Pull: A training swim that utilizes either pull buoys or paddles, or both, to improve training performance.

QS: A qualifying slot allowing an athlete to compete in a further IRONMAN race – often the IRONMAN World Championship – based on their performance in a previous IRONMAN race

RI: Recovery Interval – the length of the recovery time taken by an athlete to rest in between training intervals.

RPE: Rated Perceived Exertion – a frequently used quantitative measure of perceived exertion during physical activity, first used in the Borg RPE scale. It is used in athletics to assess the intensity of training and competition.

SA: A training swim in which the athlete swims using only a single arm, while the other arm remains at the athlete's side

SL: A training bike ride in which the athlete pedals using only a single leg, while the other leg hangs off of the bike

S+S: A training bike ride in which the athlete alternates between intervals in which they stand and sit on the bike.

Test swim: A training swim in which the athlete practices swimming at race pace.

Trainer: A training bike ride using a stationary bike.
Transition run: An easy run completed immediately following a bike workout.

WTC: The World Triathlon Corporation owns the IRONMAN brand. Founded in 1991 by Dr. James Gills with the intention of furthering the sport of triathlon, it is now owned by the Dalian Wanda Group.

WU: The warm-up portion of a training session. This should be performed at an easy level of effort.

 INDEX

(page numbers in *italic* type refer to illustrations, photos and captions)

ACKNOWLEDGEMENTS

From the inaugural race on February 18, 1978, the IRONMAN® and IRONMAN 70.3® Triathlon Series has expanded to include 154 races taking place all over the world. Through its 40 years of history, IRONMAN has developed into a company that hosts 232 standalone triathlon, running, cycling and mountain-biking events across 53 countries. With each start and finish line they cross, our athletes prove again and again that "ANYTHING IS POSSIBLE." It takes many to move mountains, however, and so we would like to acknowledge the broader IRONMAN family – one that plays a key role in the continued growth of our company and endurance sports as a whole.

Our athlete and coach community: thank you for your dedicated support, your aspiration to be the best you can be, and your drive to push the limits.

Our volunteers and local communities: thank you for your smiles and support, not only to help us put on the best races we can, but to encourage and inspire our athletes along the way.

Our partners: thank you to our corporate sponsors, charity partners, foundation partners, consumer products licensees, and vendors for creating meaningful experiences for our entire community, whether on site, in store, or across our digital channels.

Our event licensees: thank you for helping us provide superb races in communities across the globe where your resources and local expertise exceed our own.

Our employees: current and former employees and owners, we thank you for the work, the vision, and continued passion for providing life-changing experiences for our whole community.

Our original 15 who took to the shores of Waikiki and faced a challenge that many thought impossible, showing that we are only limited by our imagination.

To John and Judy Collins, for putting together a race that has changed, and continues to change, the lives and livelihood of thousands.

And last but not least, in order to put this book together with Carlton Publishing, we would like to thank Andrew Messick, Bob Babbitt, Gordon Ramsay, Lucian Randall, Jim Vance and Paula Newby-Fraser for their literary input. We would like to thank the following individuals for their fact-checking and their editing: Christopher Stadler, Dan Berglund, Colby Gorniewicz, Jennifer Ward, Ryan Lobato, Teyva Sammet, Katie Haddad, Brooks Cowan, Hilary Vander Sanden, Kyle White and Nathalie Wolderling Bishman.